The Rich
Are Different

The
R · I · C · H
Are
DIFFERENT

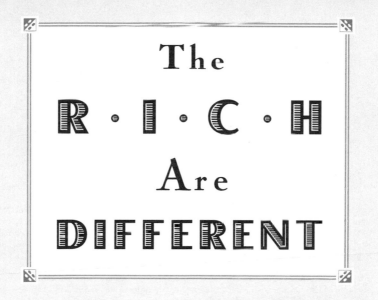

COMPILED
AND EDITED BY
JON WINOKUR

Pantheon Books
New York

Grateful acknowledgment is made to the following for permission to reprint
previously published material:

Alfred A. Knopf, Inc.: Excerpts from *Old Money* by Nelson W. Aldrich, Jr. Copyright © 1988 by Nelson W.
Aldrich, Jr. Reprinted by permission of Alfred A. Knopf, Inc. *Doubleday and Hutchinson Publishing Group:*
Excerpts from *The Big Spenders* by Lucius Beebe. Copyright © 1966 by Doubleday, a division of Bantam
Doubleday Dell. Rights in the United Kingdom administered by Hutchinson Publishing Group.
Reprinted by permission of Doubleday, a division of Bantam Doubleday Dell Publishing Group, Inc.
and the Hutchinson Publishing Group. *Grove/Atlantic, Inc.:* Excerpts from *Money and Class in America*
by Lewis Lapham. Copyright © 1988 by Lewis H. Lapham. Used by permission of Grove/Atlantic, Inc.
Little, Brown & Company: Excerpt from *The Ultra Rich* by Vance Packard. Copyright © 1989 by Vance
Packard. Reprinted by permission of Little, Brown & Company. *The Philadelphia Inquirer:* Excerpt from an
April 10, 1988, article, "The Great Taxi Giveaway" by James B. Steele and Donald L. Barlett. Copyright
© 1988 by *The Philadelphia Inquirer.* Reprinted with permission from *The Philadelphia Inquirer. Roberta Pryor,
Inc.:* Excerpt from *Class* by Paul Fussell, published by Summit Books. Copyright © 1983 by Paul Fussell.
Reprinted by permission of the author and Roberta Pryor, Inc. *Simon & Schuster, Inc. and The Renaissance
Literary Agency:* Excerpts from *Chic Savages* by John Fairchild. Copyright © 1989 by John Fairchild. Rights
in the United Kingdom administered by The Renaissance Literary Agency. Reprinted with the permission
of Simon and Schuster, Inc. and The Renaissance Literary Agency. *Warner Bros. Publications:* "The Tale of
An Oyster" by Cole Porter. Copyright © 1966, renewed 1975 by Warner Bros., Inc. All rights reserved.
Used by permission of Warner Bros. Publications U.S. Inc., Miami, FL 33014. *Yale University Press:*
Excerpts from *The Decline and Fall of the British Aristocracy* by David Cannadine. Copyright © 1990 by David
Cannadine. Reprinted by permission of Yale University Press.

Library of Congress Cataloging-in-Publication Data

The rich are different / compiled and edited by Jon Winokur.
p.   cm.
ISBN 0-679-44386-X (hc : alk. paper)
1. Money—Quotations, maxims, etc.   2. Success in business—
Quotations, maxims, etc.   3. Wealth—Quotations, maxims, etc.
4. Money—Humor.   5. Success in business—Humor.   6. Wealth—Humor.
I. Winokur, Jon.
PN6084.M56R53   1996
305.5′234—dc20   96-6258

Random House Web Address: http://www.randomhouse.com/

Book design by Deborah Kerner
Printed in the United States of America
First Edition
2 4 6 8 9 7 5 3 1

For El

Acknowledgments

I wish to thank Peter Bell, Cathy Crimmins, H. Myles Jacob, Margo Kaufman, Guy Kawasaki, Susan Nethery, Al and Betty Rasof, Beth Siniawsky, Diana Secker Larson, Jim and Nancy Steele, and Michael Wolgin for their invaluable help.

I'm especially indebted to Reid and Karen Boates, Norrie Epstein, LuAnn Walther, and Elinor Winokur for their support and encouragement.

Let me tell you about the very rich. They are different from you and me. They possess and enjoy early, and it does something to them, makes them soft where we are hard, and cynical where we are trustful, in a way that, unless you were born rich, it is difficult to understand. They think, deep in their hearts, that they are better than we are because we had to discover the compensations and refuges of life for ourselves. Even when they enter deep into our world or sink below us, they still think that they are better than we are. They are different.

F. Scott Fitzgerald, "The Rich Boy"

Contents

Introduction

"**R**ich" is an ambiguous term. J. P. Morgan said you are rich when you can "buy what you want, do what you want, and not give a damn what it costs." Henry James wrote that you are rich if you can meet the needs of your imagination. The Talmud says you are rich if you are satisfied with what you have.

Financial advisors avoid the word altogether. They describe clients with from $5 million to $20 million as having "high net worth," and anyone with more than $100 million as having "substantial wealth." (Those who have lost their fortunes are called "discontinuities.")

What was rich in the past is barely middle class today, and it is no longer true, as John Jacob Astor remarked over a century ago, that "a man who has a million dollars is as well off as if he were rich." Back then a "millionaire" was rich by definition. But what is a millionaire these days? Whereas it used to be someone with *assets* of a million dollars, a millionaire is now defined by bankers and bond salesmen as someone with an annual *income* of a million dollars.

"The rich," of course, are not monolithic. They must be classified according to the source of their wealth. There are rich inheritors whose money was made for them by somebody else; there are the rich and famous, many of whom are famous merely because they are rich; there are the rich and powerful, almost all of whom are powerful because they are rich.

Stereotypes of the rich are often true. For example, the cliché that the old rich tend to hide their wealth (page 42) and the new rich tend to flaunt it (page 60) can hardly be denied. The rich are also fussy (page 150) and extravagant (page 53); they get richer and richer (page 3), yet never seem to have enough money (page 5).

We're told repeatedly that great wealth does not make you happy, but we refuse to believe it. Yet we should believe it because, *mirabile dictu,* the rich are miserable (page 15). The more money you have, the more unhappy you will be, especially when it is left to you, as evidenced by the lives of "poor little rich kids" (page 83). The rich attract kidnappers, fortune hunters, mooches, fund-raisers, and innumerable other pests. Not only do they lack the opportunity to be Horatio Alger, they never know if they could have been even mildly successful on their own. (Unless, of course, they delude themselves— "Born on third base but thinks he hit a triple"). It isn't quite so bad if you *make* lots of money. For one thing, you're too busy to notice whether you're happy or not.

Clearly, great wealth makes its own rules no matter how it is obtained. When a pile of money reaches critical mass it explodes, shattering all proportion and producing fallout in the form of more money, also greed (page 170), arrogance (page 20), and unspeakable power (page 33).

The good news is that the rich—whether old or new, entrepreneur or inheritor, famous or infamous, all have at least one thing in common: their behavior is a spectator sport. We love to congratulate ourselves on our moral superiority to the rich. We relish the faux pas of parvenus and marvel at the chutzpah of arrivistes. Sneering at the rich is one of the few remaining forms of socially acceptable bigotry: we delight in rich people's tribulations without compunction because their wealth and privilege somehow excuse our pleasure. Guilt-free schadenfreude.

This book did not begin as an exercise in rich-bashing. Nor was it intended to be a cornucopia of wretched excess. It just turned out that way.

J. W.
Pacific Palisades, California
March 1996

Purchasing Power of a 1995 U. S. Dollar

1990	$1.16
1980	$1.85
1970	$3.92
1960	$5.14
1950	$6.32
1940	$10.87
1930	$9.11
1920	$7.61
1915	$15.07

Source: U. S. Department of Labor

The Rich
Are Different

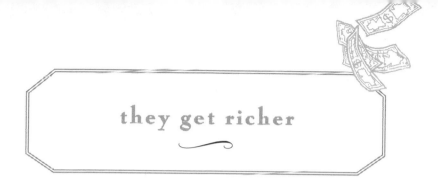

they get richer

Money is of a prolific generating nature. Money can beget money, and its offspring can beget more.

BENJAMIN FRANKLIN

The extremely wealthy, in most cases, inherit a comfortable fortune and use their power, inside knowledge, time and energy to multiply it into a grotesque one.

PHILIP SLATER

The fact that free enterprise still remains the most successful method of stimulating economic growth does not mean it requires a reward system that creates and sustains increasingly grotesque accumulations of family wealth. The accumulations are starting to have a negative influence on the efficient operation of our economy. They have the potential of being hazardous politically. And in a democratic society they are becoming inexcusable socially.

VANCE PACKARD, *The Ultra Rich*

◈ THE VERY RICH live off the income from their capital or, even better, the income from the income: Joseph P. Kennedy bought the Chicago Merchandise Mart in 1945 for $13 million; by the time he died in 1969, the annual rent exceeded that amount.

To turn $100 into $110 is work. To turn $100 million into $110 million is inevitable.

EDGAR BRONFMAN

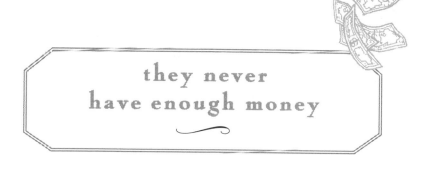

they never have enough money

Nobody ever feels rich.

ESTHER RANZEN

Although they lived in style, they felt always an anxiety in the house. There was never enough money. The mother had a small income, and the father had a small income, but not nearly enough for the social position which they had to keep up. The father went into town to some office. But though he had good prospects, these prospects never materialized. There was always the grinding sense of the shortage of money, though the style was always kept up. . . .

And so the house came to be haunted by the unspoken phrase: *There must be more money! There must be more money!* The children could hear it all the time, though nobody said it aloud. They heard it at Christmas, when the expensive and splendid toys filled the nursery. Behind the shining modern rocking-horse, behind the smart doll's-house, a voice would start whispering: "There *must* be more money! There *must* be more money!" And the children would stop playing, to listen for a moment. They would look into each other's eyes, to see if they had all heard. And each one saw in the eyes of the other that they too had heard. "There *must* be more money! There *must* be more money!"

D.H. LAWRENCE, "The Rocking-Horse Winner"

I have a beautiful weekend house in the Hamptons, but it is not, as it turns out, my summer dream house. It doesn't have the view of the ocean that I absolutely want. It doesn't have the rustic wood floors that I absolutely crave. It doesn't have a little dock to which I can tie my little rowboat. And it doesn't have the shallow water of a quiet lagoon where I can pick my plants.

MARTHA STEWART, *Interview*

William Randolph Hearst was constantly strapped despite the prodigious income from his real estate, newspaper, and mining interests. His insatiable appetite for expensive bric-a-brac (he once paid $500,000 for a pair of Cellini salt shakers), lavish entertaining, and the cost of building and maintaining San Simeon, kept him perpetually short of cash. Thus in a fabled exchange Hearst complained to Henry Ford that he never seemed to have any money: "That's a mistake," replied Ford. "A man ought to have five hundred million dollars or so in cash for a rainy day."

When a reporter asked him to confirm the speculation that he was worth over a billion dollars, J. Paul Getty thought for a moment and replied, "Yes, I suppose it's true, but a billion dollars doesn't go as far as it used to."

The Newport spinster Edith Wetmore, who died in 1966, didn't enter a grocery store until she was over eighty, when a friend took her to an A&P. After shopping the aisles, she wheeled her cart to a check-out counter, but Miss Wetmore, whose income was $6,000 a day, did not have a cent in her purse so her friend had to pay.

At lunch that day with Secretary of the Treasury Ogden L. Mills, someone had raised the question of how much one could live on comfortably. Someone else had timidly suggested $50,000 a year, whereupon Mills replied with open scorn, "On $50,000 a year you can't even keep clean."

      JOSEPH W. ALSOP, *I've Seen the Best of It*

A young Nelson Rockefeller was sailing his toy boat in a pond when another boy asked, "Where's your yacht?"

"Whaddaya think I am," he replied, "a Vanderbilt?"

When an elderly John D. Rockefeller, Sr., learned that members of his family intended to give him an electric cart to aid him in getting around his estate, he told them, "If you don't mind, I'd rather have the money."

they never have enough money

The Laws of Money

Money is the seed of money, and the first guinea is sometimes more difficult to acquire than the second million.

JEAN JACQUES ROUSSEAU

The force of the guinea you have in your pocket depends wholly on the default of a guinea in your neighbor's pocket. If he did not want it, it would be of no use to you.

JOHN RUSKIN

Money is like water: Too little creates a desert, too much a flood. Only in the right proportions does it give life.

JUDITH GREEN

Money is like muck, not good except it be spread.

FRANCIS BACON

People will swim through shit if you put a few bob in it.

PETER SELLERS

Money is a terrible master but an excellent servant.

P. T. BARNUM

L'or, même à la laideur, donne un teint de beauté.
Gold lends a touch of beauty even to the ugly.

NICOLAS BOILEAU

Time is money.

BENJAMIN FRANKLIN

Money is a singular thing. It ranks with love as man's greatest source of joy. And with death as his greatest source of anxiety. Money differs from an automobile, a mistress or cancer in being equally important to those who have it and those who do not.

JOHN KENNETH GALBRAITH

The chief value of money lies in the fact that one lives in a world in which it is overestimated.

H. L. MENCKEN

Money is what you'd get on beautifully without if only other people weren't so crazy about it.

MARGARET CASE HARRIMAN

Nothing that is God's is obtainable by money.

TERTULLIAN

The Laws of Money

When it is a question of money, everyone is of the same religion.

VOLTAIRE

If women didn't exist, all the money in the world would have no meaning.

ARISTOTLE ONASSIS

To have subsidized a Bach, or Fulbrighted a Beethoven, would have done no good at all. Money may kindle but it cannot, by itself, and for very long, burn.

IGOR STRAVINSKY

Money is applause.

JACQUELINE SUSANN

Money is round. It rolls away.

SHOLEM ALEICHEM

Money is human happiness *in abstracto*; consequently he who is no longer capable of happiness *in concreto* sets his whole heart on money.

ARTHUR SCHOPENHAUER

Anyone who thinks money will make you happy . . . hasn't got money. . . . Happy is harder than money.

DAVID GEFFEN

Money doesn't make you happy, but it quiets the nerves.

SEAN O'CASEY

Money brings some happiness. But, after a certain point, it just brings more money.

NEIL SIMON

Money can't make you happy, but unless you have money, you can't make that statement.

BERRY GORDY

Money is like a sixth sense without which you cannot make a complete use of the other five.

W. SOMERSET MAUGHAM

Money cannot buy peace of mind, greatness of spirit, serenity, confidence, or self-sufficiency.

PLUTARCH

Money buys everything except love, personality, freedom, immortality, silence, peace.

CARL SANDBURG

Money can't buy friends, but you can get a better class of enemy.

SPIKE MILLIGAN

Money is only important if you don't have it. I've been broke lots of times in my life, but I've never been poor.

MIKE TODD

When I was young I thought money was the most important thing in life; now that I am old I know that it is.

OSCAR WILDE

Money isn't everything as long as you have enough.

MALCOLM FORBES

Those who have some means think that the most important thing in the world is love. The poor know that it is money.

GERALD BRENAN

Money is better than poverty, if only for financial reasons.

WOODY ALLEN

To be clever enough to get a great deal of money, one must be stupid enough to want it.

G. K. CHESTERTON

If you're going to make money, you have to look like money.

JAMES BUCHANAN "DIAMOND JIM" BRADY

It is true that money attracts; but much money repels.

CYNTHIA OZICK

It isn't enough for you to love money—it's also necessary that money should love you.

BARON JAMES DE ROTHSCHILD

Money is the root of every mess you can think of.

SADIE AND BESSIE DELANY

We all know how the size of sums of money appears to vary in a remarkable way according as they being paid in or paid out.

JULIAN HUXLEY

Creditors have better memories than debtors.

BENJAMIN FRANKLIN

A billion here, a billion there—pretty soon it adds up to real money.

SENATOR EVERETT DIRKSEN

You must spend money if you wish to make money.

PLAUTUS

When a fellow says it isn't the money but the principle of the thing, it's the money.

KIN HUBBARD

Money talks. The more money, the louder it talks.

ARNOLD ROTHSTEIN

Money doesn't talk anymore, it shrieks.

SUZY (AILEEN MEHLE)

When a person with money meets a person with experience, the person with the experience winds up with the money and the person with the money winds up with the experience.

HARVEY MACKAY

Money is like fire, an element as little troubled by moralizing as earth, air and water. Men can employ it as a tool or they can dance around it as if it were the incarnation of a god. Money votes socialist or monarchist, finds a profit in pornography or translations from the Bible, commissions Rembrandt and underwrites the technology of Auschwitz. It acquires its meaning from the uses to which it is put.

LEWIS H. LAPHAM

Money follows different laws from the rest of nature. Money goes where it will increase fastest rather than where it's needed, and it has no national loyalties.

JOSEPH HELLER

As a cousin of mine once said about money, money is always there but the pockets change; it is not in the same pockets after a change, and that is all there is to say about money.

GERTRUDE STEIN

they're miserable

A great fortune is a great slavery.

SENECA

At the poverty level money tends to *increase* the options available to us (both for pleasure and for relief from pain), while at the level of affluence money tends to *decrease* the options available to us.

PHILIP SLATER

Golden shackles are far worse than iron ones.

GANDHI

A gilded life may, in many ways, become a gilded cage.

CLAUS VON BÜLOW, a few days after being acquitted of the attempted murder of his wife

Money brings me nothing but a certain dull anxiety.

JOHN JACOB ASTOR III

Hetty Green (1834–1916) owned a little mutt that was a chronic biter. When one of the dog's victims suggested she get rid of it, the reclusive multimillionairess replied, "I know, I know, but he loves me and doesn't know how rich I am."

If I had my life to live over again I'd be a thirty-dollar-a-week librarian.

ANDREW CARNEGIE

If I hadn't been rich, I might have been a really great man.

ORSON WELLES as Charles Foster Kane in *Citizen Kane* (screenplay by Herman Mankiewicz and Orson Welles)

The best reason to read about the very rich, of course, is to be reassured that money cannot buy happiness—and, indeed, often seems to buy trouble.

MAUREEN DOWD

There is always the question. You wonder if people like you for you—or the inevitable disturbing question: "Are they after something?"

MARY LEA JOHNSON, heir to the Johnson & Johnson fortune

Who, outside the family, wanted nothing from him but friendship? Who admired and liked him for himself alone? Nelson's grandfather had once explained his few golfing partners: "I have made experiments, and nearly always the result is the same. Along about the ninth hole comes some proposition charitable or financial."

JOSEPH PERSICO, *The Imperial Rockefeller*

I don't care whether I win or lose, and when you can't enjoy winning at poker, there's no fun left in anything.

JOHN MACKAY, THE "COMSTOCK SILVER KING"

Where there is too much, something is missing.

LEO ROSTEN

Luxury is more deadly than any foe.

JUVENAL

In some ways, a millionaire just can't win. If he spends too freely, he is criticized for being extravagant and ostentatious. If, on the other hand, he lives quietly and thriftily, the same people who would have criticized him for being profligate will call him a miser.

J. PAUL GETTY

The rich who are unhappy are worse off than the poor who are unhappy; for the poor at least cling to the hope that more money would solve their problems, but the rich know better.

SIDNEY HARRIS

they're miserable

The man with a toothache thinks everyone happy whose teeth are sound. The poverty stricken man makes the same mistake about the rich man.

GEORGE BERNARD SHAW, *Maxims for Revolutionists*

While thinking they always win, the rich actually lose twice: once while they're alive, because with so much to lose they never really take chances; and once when they die, because being rich they lose so much.

JERZY KOSINSKI

To suppose, as we all suppose, that we could be rich and not behave as the rich behave, is like supposing that we could drink all day and stay sober.

LOGAN PEARSALL SMITH

❖ MANY RICH PEOPLE require their employees to sign nondisclosure agreements swearing them to secrecy about everything they observe while employed.

❖ ACCORDING TO HER biographer Stephanie Mansfield, Doris Duke kept a squad of private investigators on constant retainer "for general snooping purposes," and had all her mail shredded and scattered in separate waste baskets.

❖ H. ROSS PEROT reportedly had an underling posing as a journalist call Mrs. Perot to see if she would reveal confidential matters. (She did.)

❖ IN COLOMBIA, WHERE the wealthy are in constant danger of being kidnapped by leftist guerrillas, rich kids don't brag about their cars or their houses, but about their bodyguards.

[Howard] Hughes . . . started as a very presentable young playboy with the world at his disposal, and ended as a starving, paranoid recluse trapped in a room watching old movies. Nor is this uncommon among the very rich: wealthy, paranoid, depressed recluses are a dime a dozen—Hughes was simply more theatrical about it, a result, perhaps, of his years in Hollywood.

PHILIP SLATER

As time goes on I find myself thinking more and more about Howard Hughes and even, to some degree, identifying with him. Take, for example, his famous aversion to germs. While I'm certainly not as fanatical as he was, I've always had strong feelings about cleanliness. I'm constantly washing my hands.

DONALD TRUMP, *Survival at the Top*

they're miserable

they're arrogant

◆ HENRY FORD II's estranged second wife Cristina once told an interviewer that while shaving he would look in the mirror and say, "I am the king. The king can do no wrong." After Ford was arrested for drunk driving in the company of a woman not (but who later became) his wife, he was convicted and sentenced to two years' probation. To the crowd of reporters outside the courthouse, he would say only, "Never complain, never explain," a phrase he adopted as his personal motto.

◆ WHEN ISABELLA STEWART (Mrs. Jack) Gardner of Boston hired Paderewski to play at afternoon tea for herself and a friend, she insisted that the great pianist and composer stay hidden behind a screen.

◆ _____

When the aristocratic Mrs. Stuyvesant Fish (who once explained, "We are not rich, we only have a few million") and her husband got up to leave a dinner party early,

Harry Lehr (an impudent upstart who once told a diamond-bedecked Mrs. Astor that she looked like a chandelier) shouted from across the room, "Sit down, Fishes, you're not rich enough to leave first."

◈

◈ AFTER THREE OF his top subordinates were killed in a helicopter crash in 1989, Donald Trump claimed he had been scheduled to fly with them but canceled at the last minute. In fact, according to his biographer John R. O'Donnell, Trump had never intended to take the flight.

◈ THE OIL BILLIONAIRE H. L. Hunt wrote and published a book in which he proposed that citizens' voting power be proportionate to the amount of taxes they paid.

◈ FLORENCE VANDERBILT TWOMBLY steadfastly refused to recognize Labor Day as a holiday.

◈ H. ROSS PEROT had a coral reef dynamited at his oceanfront home in Bermuda because it interfered with his boat slip.

◈

Jerome Zipkin, who died in 1995 at the age of eighty, was a wealthy Manhattan real estate heir who devoted his adult life to escorting such prominent women as Betsy Bloomingdale, Estée Lauder, Pat Buckley, and Nancy Reagan to an endless round of functions, earning him the gossip-column appellations "social moth" and "walker." His notoriously short temper earned him the enmity of service personnel everywhere: one close friend kept a ready supply of $20 bills to placate waiters and taxi drivers he

they're arrogant

had insulted. But Zipkin's wrath was not restricted to the help. Once at a luncheon a waiter asked if he could do anything for him, and Zipkin replied, "You can remove the lady on my right."

◈ WHEN JOHN D. MACARTHUR, the Florida land developer and founder of the foundation which awards "genius grants" was attacked by environmentalists during the 1970s, he dismissed them as "bearded jerks and little old ladies" and asked, "Has anyone ever justified the existence of an alligator? . . . Let's stuff a few and put them in a museum and get rid of the rest."

One of the greatest delusions of the superrich is that wealth bestows wisdom. This notion is especially beguiling when the superrich begin with nothing and wind up building companies, employing people, and changing the course of industries, purely on the strength of their ideas and their acumen. After a while—after they've gone against the grain a dozen times and been proved right; after they've gotten used to hearing everyone they come in contact with tell them how great they are—they succumb to the all-too-natural tendency to believe they are, indeed, infallible. And as they grow older and find there is nothing left to conquer in business, they often begin thinking something else: that the real reason they were put on this earth was not to build a better mousetrap but to save the world.

JOSEPH NOCERA, *GQ*

Years ago, my father overheard this exchange in a club. A man who was listening to another tell a rather long-winded story suddenly stopped a passing waiter and said, "Would you mind listening to the rest of this man's story; I have somewhere to go," and he got up to leave.

LANG PHIPPS, *New York Magazine*

◈ ARMAND HAMMER BOUGHT an important manuscript by Leonardo da Vinci and renamed it the *Codex Hammer.*

◈ LEE IACOCCA CUT merit pay for Chrysler employees while accepting $20 million in compensation for himself, explaining: "That's the American way. If little kids don't aspire to make money like I did, what the hell good is this country?"

◈ WHEN MRS. JOHN GUTFREUND (a former flight attendant who married one of New York's wealthiest financiers) decided to throw a memorable party, she rented Blenheim Palace in England and sent out engraved invitations which read: "Mr. and Mrs. John Gutfreund, At Home, Blenheim."

A woman needs four animals in her life: A mink in the closet. A jaguar in the garage. A tiger in bed. And an ass to pay for it all.

ANNE SLATER

they're arrogant

I am the richest man in the world. I am worth $194 million. I would not walk across the street to make a million dollars.

WILLIAM K. VANDERBILT

In March of 1898, William Randolph Hearst dispatched the artist Frederic Remington to Havana to cover the "war" with Cuba, but soon after he arrived, Remington cabled Hearst complaining that there was no action to be found and could he please return home. Hearst immediately cabled back: YOU FURNISH THE PICTURES AND I'LL FURNISH THE WAR.

I have no complex about wealth. I have worked hard for my money, producing things people need. I believe that the able industrial leader who creates wealth and employment is more worthy of historical notice than politicians and soldiers.

J. PAUL GETTY

Everybody ought to be rich.

JOHN JACOB RASKOB

The Pittsburgh steel baron Andrew Mellon was then [in 1931] serving as secretary of the treasury under President Hoover. Mellon, whose vast fortune no candyass Great Depression could dent, was an advocate of the fuck-it school of economic philosophy: "Liquidate labor, liquidate stocks, liquidate the farmer, liquidate real estate." Let the damned thing take its natural course, and to hell with handouts.

"People will work harder, live a more moral life. Values will be adjusted, and enterprising people will pick up the wrecks from less competent people."

NICK TOSCHES, *Dino*

When a socialist harangued Andrew Carnegie about redistribution of wealth, Carnegie asked his secretary for two numbers—the world's population and the value of all his assets. He divided the latter by the former, then said to his secretary, "Give this gentleman 16 cents. That is his share of my net worth."

GEORGE WILL

This has been said many times, and I strongly believe it—if you took all the money in the world and distributed it amongst all the people, within x amount of time—five years, three years, six months—the rich would be rich, and the poor would be poor. Why? Because some people know how to play Monopoly, and some people don't know how to play Monopoly.

DAVID MARSHALL, a wealthy real estate developer

What's invidious about these careless people is their sense of composure, as though they were perfectly integrated in spirit, mind, and body. Nowhere in their makeup, it seems, are there any of those embarrassing dissonances of motive, those deformities of character or bewildering blanks in sensibility, that afflict the more common run of men and women. Seymour St. John, Choate's longtime headmaster, caught the essence of this quality in a phrase: "the sheer restfulness of good breeding," he called it. Such people are whole where others are in pieces; they are smooth where others are coarse; they are broad where others are narrow. Above all, they are confident, fearless, gallant—the adjectives fell like rose petals around the three Roosevelts, for example, and John F. Kennedy—when everyone else is weak, hesitant, fearful, or ashamed.

NELSON W. ALDRICH, JR., *Old Money*

Badgered by a reporter that the public had a right to know why he had closed a money-losing passenger line, William K. Vanderbilt, the head of the New York Central Railroad, replied, "The public be damned! I am working for my stockholders."

SEC investigators found Boesky and Milken contemptuous of the federal government when questioned about their activities. That morning at SEC headquarters in Washington, after Boesky sat down at a small conference table for his interrogation concerning suspicious trades he had made in the shares of the soft drink company Dr. Pepper, the financier exceeded his considerable reputation for arrogance.

Boesky pulled a cigar from his suit-coat pocket. Before he could light it, one of the SEC lawyers told him to put it away.

"I have a right to smoke my cigar," Boesky said.

"We'd appreciate it if you didn't," an SEC lawyer responded. "This is a small conference room and some of us are allergic to smoke."

"I have a right to smoke if I want to," Boesky declared.

"Please, as a courtesy, we ask you not to smoke."

"I ask, as a courtesy, that you allow me to smoke," Boesky said, and turned to Henry King. "Counsel, I ask that you demand my right to smoke."

King appeared to be embarrassed. "My client would like to smoke," he said, repeating the obvious.

And so Ivan Boesky lit his cigar and began to fill the room with blue-gray smoke, even before the SEC lawyers could ask their first question of him.

DAVID A. VISE AND STEVE COLL, *Washington Post*

Emanuel Ungaro . . . recalled the Duchess [of Windsor] in her heyday, maintaining her title as perennially best-dressed woman by ordering magnificent clothes and never paying a bill. Balenciaga had been the first to call it quits. He dispatched Ungaro, then a young designer and assistant, to the house in the Bois with a coat in a box and an ultimatum, staggering in its *lèse-majesté:* no check, no coat. Ungaro rang the doorbell and gave the message but not the coat to the servant who answered. The door was shut in his face. Presently it opened again, just a crack, and a hand with a check appeared around the edge. He took the check, presented the box to the Duchess—in person—and fled. She continued to wear clothes from Balenciaga, at that time the finest living designer, and he went on withholding them until he was paid on the nail. It was Ungaro who had to oversee the fittings. Blaming the messenger, the Duchess snubbed him, which is the truly uncivil part of the story. She would stand before the mirror and silently point to a seam she wanted altered. A bold player, a petty loser; a way of life.

MAVIS GALLANT, *Times Literary Supplement*

The greatest political stylist the world has ever known was Mrs. Eva Perón. The crowning moment of her entire career was when she rose in her box in the opera house in Buenos Aires to make a speech. She lifted her hands to the crowd, and as she did so, with a sound like railway coaches in a siding, the diamond bracelets slid from her wrists to her armpits. When the expensive clatter had died away, her speech began, "We, the shirtless . . ."

QUENTIN CRISP, *How to Have a Life-Style*

I can remove all the Constitutional Scruples in the District of Columbia [with] half a dozen presidencies, a dozen cashierships, fifty clerkships, and 100 directorships to worthy friends who have no character and no money.

NICHOLAS BIDDLE

What do I care about the law? Hain't I got the power?

CORNELIUS VANDERBILT

The rules are . . . there are no rules.

ARISTOTLE ONASSIS

Janet Jackson is one hot number. Everybody thinks so. Including, and perhaps most lavishly, a prince of Saudi Arabia. Recently, this prince invited Janet and her beau, René Elizondo, to a deluxe dinner in L.A. He was gracious to Elizondo, but it was soon uncomfortably clear that the prince had big eyes and even bigger designs on Janet.

After dining with Janet and René, the prince sent word immediately that he wanted to do it again. Only this time he wanted Janet alone. But—get this—he said that to make up for any "inconvenience" to René, he would buy Janet's guy "the gift of your choice." And the prince made it clear that whatever René's choice was, he was willing to pay big-time for the privilege of spending hours alone with Janet. When René and Janet said thanks but no thanks, the prince then offered to contribute heavily to René's favorite charity.

René declined, sending the firm and final word that he and Miss Jackson would be unavailable for any further dinners—á deux or trois!

LIZ SMITH, *Los Angeles Times*

The biography his office gave me starts: "Dr. Samuel J. LeFrak is a distinguished business leader, scientist, developer, builder, urban expert, yachtsman, patron of the arts, philanthropist and humanitarian . . . an experienced statesman."

Whenever LeFrak's secretary called she stated: "Dr. LeFrak would like to speak with you."

they're arrogant

The doctorate is strictly an honorary one from a college where he has been a trustee.

VANCE PACKARD, *The Ultra Rich*

In the struggle for power
O the scramble for pelf
Let this be your motto
Rely on yourself

SAMUEL J. LEFRAK, a New York real estate developer who inherited his father's construction company

When someone asked Hetty Green to recommend a good investment, the "Witch of Wall Street" replied, "The other world."

When a man accosted him on the street and asked, "What's the market going to do?" J. P. Morgan replied, "It will fluctuate."

It's a matter of having principles. It's easy to have principles when you're rich. The important thing is to have principles when you're poor.

RAY KROC

When I was a girl we were comparatively poor, but still much richer than most of the world, and when I married I became very rich. It used to worry me, and I thought it wrong to have so many beautiful things when others had nothing. Now I realize that it is possible for the rich to sin by coveting the privileges of the poor. The poor have always been favorites of God and His saints, but I believe it is one of the special achievements of Grace to sanctify the whole of life, riches included. Wealth in pagan Rome was necessarily something cruel; it's not anymore.

LADY MARCHMAIN IN EVELYN WAUGH'S *Brideshead Revisited*

A man who has $200,000 is about as well off, for all practical purposes, as I am.

H. L. HUNT (circa 1950)

I wish to become so rich that I can instruct the people and glorify honest poverty a little, like those kindhearted, fat, benevolent people do.

MARK TWAIN

To me one of the most exciting things in the world is being poor. Survival is such an exciting challenge. There was a study done about twenty years ago, I think at Harvard, which said that the average family of four could live on $68 a year. That's a balanced diet—everything they need for a year. Now today that might be $250 or $300, but when we see these people in line in supermarkets with all these food stamps, buying potato chips and snack foods and ice cream, I mean, give me a break! *That's* poverty?

TOM MONAGHAN, founder of Domino's Pizza

they're arrogant

I believe the power to make money is a gift from God.

JOHN D. ROCKEFELLER

"It was beautiful, they looked great," said Malcolm Serure, who said he was a best friend of the groom [at the wedding of Prince Alexandre Egon von und zu Fürstenberg and Alexandra Natasha Miller]. Asked what he did for a living, he paused quizzically.

"What do I *do?*" he parroted. "Investing."

CAREY GOLDBERG, *New York Times*

The insolence of wealth will creep out.

SAMUEL JOHNSON

The Rich Are Different

they have clout

Rich men without convictions are more dangerous in modern society than poor women without chastity.

GEORGE BERNARD SHAW

THE POET HEINRICH HEINE was a friend of the Rothschild family, even though he never hid his contempt for their wealth. He once said of Baron James de Rothschild, "Money is the God of our time, and Rothschild is his prophet." Heine also noted the baron's effect on others: "I have seen people who on approaching the great baron shudder as if they had touched an electric current."

A million or two is as much as anyone ought to have, but what you have is not worth anything unless you have the power. And if you give away the surplus, you give away the control.

CORNELIUS VANDERBILT

WHEN HENRY M. FLAGLER, John D. Rockefeller's most famous partner and a pioneer Florida real estate developer, had his first wife committed to a mental asylum and attempted to dissolve their marriage, he discovered that Florida law excluded insanity as grounds for divorce. The Florida legislature, in apparent gratitude for Flagler's previous largesse, quickly passed a law validating insanity as grounds for divorce, Flagler legally rid himself of the unfortunate woman, and the legislature immediately repealed what became known as "Flagler's Law."

A down-on-his-luck trader came to Baron Rothschild for a loan. After listening patiently to the man's sob story, the baron replied that he wouldn't lend him money, but that he'd do something better, whereupon he took the man to the London Stock Exchange and walked with him arm-in-arm across the trading floor.

After her sentencing . . . to a four-year prison term, Leona Helmsley spent four days in a private room at New York Hospital, a hospital to which she had pledged $33 million. The doctors there were very concerned about her health. Her personal doctor declared there would be a "fatal determination," if Leona had to go to jail. No one I have met knows what "a fatal determination" is supposed to mean.

DENNIS DUGGAN, *Newsday*

Whenever he was in Monte Carlo, which was frequently, the newspaper magnate James Gordon Bennett (1841–1918) always dined on mutton chops at the same table at the same restaurant. One evening the table was occupied, so the outraged Bennett immediately bought the restaurant for $40,000, commanded all the customers to leave, sat down and took his customary meal, and then gave the deed to the waiter as a tip. (The waiter's name was Ciro, and he became an internationally acclaimed restaurateur.)

James Gordon Bennett once proposed a British cavalry officer for membership in the Reading Room, a tony but hidebound Newport men's club. Bennett persuaded the officer to ride a horse into the library of the club, to the utter chagrin of its dozing denizens. When the board predictably rejected his friend's application, Bennett resigned in a huff, purchased a plot of land nearby, hired the architect Stanford White, and built a club of his own, the Newport Casino.

they have clout

A former Mrs. Vanderbilt . . . told me it was a hard name to surrender, even for a subsequent marriage, so great were the perks throughout the world for anyone called Mrs. Vanderbilt. No restaurant anywhere, however crowded, she said, declines a reservation from someone bearing that lustrous name.

DOMINICK DUNNE, *Vanity Fair*

During the 1950s, a young geologist named Charles Steen took his family to a remote section of Utah to prospect for uranium. As the months passed without a strike, his money ran out and the family often went hungry. But Steen persevered, finally striking a rich vein of ore that made him a millionaire. One of the first things he bought with his new wealth was the bank in Colorado that had once refused him a $200 loan.

Transatlantic passengers aboard the *Berengaria*, the *Paris*, or *Rotterdam* in the 1920s became familiar with a personable and very stout French gentleman who traveled the sea lanes on his business occasions named Count La Riboissier. An affable and chatty member of the international set, the Count carried considerable sums of money about his person at all times and in all national currencies. He had, he disclosed to smoke-room acquaintances, about him whenever he was away from home the equivalent of $1,000 each in pounds, francs, guilders, zloty, milreis, taler, yen, pesos, marks, pengö, drachmas, and the like, perhaps a total of $10,000 in all the currencies of the then traveled world. Invariably friends would ask why he exposed himself thus to possible robbery when traveler's checks were so much handier?

"It is this way," said Count La Riboissier. "I am, as you see, a fat man, nearly twenty stone on the hoof, and one day I am in a public café in Rio de Janeiro when a young lady acquaintance stops to give me good day. Chivalry is not dead. I leap to my feet and I break a leg in so doing. I have no appreciable money on me so they throw me in the public pest house. You have never been in a city hospital in Rio de Janeiro? A good thing. It is deplorable. So now wherever I am, I carry ample money of that country to be able to break a leg in ten languages. I am then a first-class street accident."

LUCIUS BEEBE, *The Big Spenders*

During the 1890s, when William Randolph Hearst's New York Journal *was engaged in a costly circulation war with Joseph Pulitzer's* World, *an accountant warned Hearst that he was losing a million dollars a year. Hearst thought for a moment and replied, "At that rate I can only last another thirty years."*

One day in the 1830s, in the anteroom of Baron James de Rothschild's Paris banking office, the German poet Heinrich Heine observed this scene: when a servant emerged from the baron's inner sanctum carrying a chamber pot, a speculator waiting for an appointment rose to his feet, lifted his hat, and bowed solemnly as the rich man's excreta went by.

Every child of Old Money grows up under a barrage of verbal snow-balls impugning his or her personal powers. A rich kid is a kid who can't boil an egg, comb her own hair, wear the same sweater twice, balance her checkbook, wash the dishes, take the subway, do the laundry, eat with her fingers, lift a finger, change a flat tire, fight his way out of a wet paper bag, bicycle to school, go out with the guys, tie his own shoelaces, mow the lawn, stand up for his rights, stand being hurt, stand on his own two feet.

NELSON W. ALDRICH, JR., *Old Money*

When the profligate duke of Devonshire found himself besieged by creditors, his financial advisors proposed various domestic economies, including the suggestion that he might possibly be able to get along without three nationalities of pastry chef (French, Viennese, and Danish), to which the indignant duke replied, "Good Lord, can't a man have a biscuit if he wants it?"

When the duke of Marlborough could no longer afford his valet, who had, among other things, always put the paste on the duke's toothbrush, the nobleman's shock was palpable: "What's the matter with my toothbrush?" he exclaimed. "The damned thing won't foam anymore!"

Until the age of twelve I sincerely believed that everybody had a house on Fifth Avenue, a villa in Newport and a steam-driven, ocean-going yacht.

CORNELIUS VANDERBILT, JR.

[It's] nothing but what a reasonable and practical family may live up to . . . the vision and image of a typical American residence.

WILLIAM K. VANDERBILT, of his fifty-eight-room Fifth Avenue mansion

I have had no real gratification or enjoyment of any sort more than my neighbor on the next block who is worth only half a million.

WILLIAM K. VANDERBILT, who was worth $200 million when he died in 1885

When Baron Sackville-West, who lived on a large estate in Kent, was told that a friend had recently acquired a dog, he replied, "But how can he keep a dog? He hasn't got a park to walk it in."

During [Nelson Rockefeller's] campaign for the presidency in 1968 I remember him making a speech to a crowd of Puerto Rican steelworkers in a slum near Cleveland, Ohio. Exuding his familiar optimism, his arms raised in a gesture of brotherhood, Rockefeller addressed the crowd in well-meaning Spanish, promising that if he was elected President of the United States he would do everything in his power to distribute justice, fiscal responsibility and pieces of the American pie. The crowd cheered him with shouts of *"Arriba, Arriba,"* never knowing, as the candidate himself didn't know, that Rockefeller owned the steel mill.

LEWIS H. LAPHAM, *Money and Class in America*

On a visit to the Holy Land in 1887, Edmond de Rothschild, upon seeing the Wailing Wall in Jerusalem for the first time, calmly inquired if it might be for sale.

One day as a young child, Marie Thérèse Charlotte, Duchesse d'Angoulême (1778– 1851) and daughter of Louis XVI and Marie Antoinette, was playing with a servant, and suddenly noticing the woman's hands, she exclaimed, "Why, you have five fingers, just like me!"

Mr. Podsnap was well to do, and stood very high in Mr. Podsnap's opinion. Beginning with a good inheritance, he had married into a good inheritance, and had thriven exceedingly in the Marine Insurance way, and was quite satisfied. He never could make out why everybody was not quite satisfied, and he felt conscious that he set a brilliant social example in being particularly satisfied with most things, and, above all other things, with himself.

CHARLES DICKENS, *Our Mutual Friend*

While controversy was raging over *The Bell Curve*, which contends that intelligence among blacks is immutably lower than among whites, there was some speculation that I planned to write a book demonstrating that rich people from Social Register backgrounds are, for the most part, dumb as dirt. I want to make it clear that I have no such plans.

CALVIN TRILLIN, *New York Times Magazine*

Survivors of the years of the ortolans at Bar Harbor such as Colonel Haskell H. Cleaves, a retired army officer, remember the high point in Ed Stotesbury's career as one of the three or four undisputed grandees of the American resort scene. The occasion was in honor of the banker's eightieth birthday when a small dinner was given for him at the Bar Harbor Club in August 1929. "I have today achieved my life's ambition," Stotesbury told those present with all the pride of a small boy who had been honored by the members of his high-school class. "I have just received a letter from my financial advisor telling me I am worth a hundred million dollars."

Life could hold no more.

LUCIUS BEEBE, *The Big Spenders*

they don't have a clue

Old Money

Caroline Astor—known as *the* Mrs. Astor—was the grandest of the grande dames. She decreed that it took three generations of wealth untainted by work "in trade" to qualify for social acceptability. As she put it, the money had to "cool off."

JAN TUCKWOOD, *Palm Beach Post*

WHAT ERNEST DIDN'T KNOW
Old money's not the same as new.
Old money owns a family pew,
Saves string, soap slivers and eschews
New frocks at St. Bartholemew's.
New money makes old money twitch.
Old money never mentions "rich,"
A nuance lost on Ernest when
God knows Scott could have used a ten.

W. H. VON DREELE

Prior to the Reagan era, the newly rich aped the old rich. But that isn't true any longer. Donald Trump is making no effort to behave like Eleanor Roosevelt as far as I can see.

FRAN LEBOWITZ

Gentility is what is left over from rich ancestors after the money is gone.

JOHN CIARDI

The difference between old veau and nouveau is that one dies, and the other buys.

BEAUREGARD HOUSTON-MONTGOMERY, *Details*

As a class indicator the amount of money is less significant than the source. The main thing distinguishing the top three classes from each other is the amount of money inherited in relation to the amount currently earned. The top-out-of-sight class (Rockefellers, Pews, DuPonts, Mellons, Fords, Vanderbilts) lives on inherited capital entirely. No one whose money, no matter how copious, comes from his own work—film stars are an example—can be a member of the top-out-of-sight class, even if the size of his income and the extravagance of his expenditure permit him to simulate identity with it. Inheritance—"old money" in the vulgar phrase—is the indispensable principle defining the top three classes, and it's best if the money's been in the family for three or four generations. There are subtle local ways to ascertain how long the money's been there. Touring middle America, the British traveller Jonathan Raban came upon the girl Sally, who informed him that "New Money says Missouri; Old Money says Missoura."

PAUL FUSSELL, *Class*

One cannot exaggerate Old Money's fear of loss. It poisons their most salient virtues, and it poisons the whole aim of their schools' Periclean ordeal, which is to induce in their children a gift of the self to the public world. The anxiety of the trust-fund rich over the market, the fear of the clubman for his privacy, the dread of poor little rich girls for bounders and cads, the uneasiness of the contented in the face of the hungry—all these apprehensions settle easily into one of the most persuasive convictions of the Old Rich: that the world is out to take advantage of them.

NELSON W. ALDRICH, JR., *Old Money*

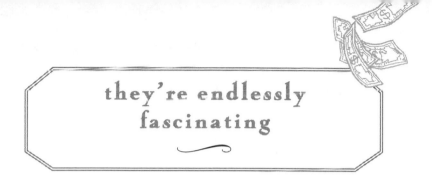

they're endlessly fascinating

The mystique of wealth [is] the ultimate magnet—and the greater the fortune, the more unimaginable and mythical its dimensions, the more compelling its attraction.

CARY REICH, Financier, *The Biography of André Meyer*

People are fascinated by the rich: Shakespeare wrote plays about kings, not beggars.

DOMINICK DUNNE

There's nothing that the public likes more than the rich and the powerful in a criminal situation.

MICHAEL KORDA (quoted by Dominick Dunne)

With money in your pocket you are wise, you are handsome, and you sing well, too.

YIDDISH PROVERB

Throughout the world people love fairy tales, especially related to the lives of the rich. You must learn to understand this and accept it.

ARISTOTLE ONASSIS to Jacqueline Kennedy

All heiresses are beautiful.

JOHN DRYDEN

No rich man is ugly.

ZSA ZSA GABOR

they're stingy

She never tipped bellboys, porters, taxi drivers or hotel maids. Instead, she carried with her a supply of specially printed cards, about the size of a postcard, that had a picture of President Kennedy on the front and some of his favorite passages of Scripture on the back, along with the famous line from his inaugural address, "Ask not what your country can do for you; ask what you can do for your country." She autographed these cards and handed them out in lieu of tips, saying blithely, "Save this; someday it will be worth money."

BARBARA GIBSON, *Life with Rose Kennedy*

My daily lunch at Boston's Kenmore Square was a tuna fish sandwich and a milkshake. My continuous patronage of his establishment was sometimes acknowledged by a nod from Mr. Brudno, the proprietor. On one memorable occasion Mr. Joe Kennedy, multi-millionaire progenitor of *the* Kennedys, climbed onto the stool beside me. I noted that he also ordered a milkshake with his sandwich. As I was half-turned, better to observe my eminent lunch companion, I could see Mr. Brudno in back of us pointing at Mr. Kennedy and mouthing to the counter person, "No check for Mr. Kennedy." Mr. Kennedy finished his lunch, seemed not surprised at the lack of a check, shook Mr. Brudno's extended hand, and left. As I paid my check Mr. Brudno, presumably still overcome by the presence of his illustrious guest, did not nod.

HENRY EPSTEIN

The man who tips a shilling every time he stops for petrol is giving away annually the cost of lubricating his car.

J. PAUL GETTY

Lord Nathan Rothschild was scolded by a hansom cab driver for an inadequate tip: "Your lordship's son usually gives me a much larger sum," said the driver. "Ah," replied Lord Rothschild, "that's because he has a rich father and I haven't."

It's rude and inconsiderate to overtip. It only makes it more difficult—and embarrassing—for people who are not as rich as I am.

J. PAUL GETTY

To describe the rich as people is often to make a mistake with the language. Rich nouns or pronouns, perhaps, but not people. The rich tend to identify themselves with a sum of money, and by so doing they relinquish most of their claims to their own humanity. Their money becomes a synthetic fabrication of heart and mind, an artificial circulatory system. This is why it is so difficult to borrow from the rich, why they forget to pay their bills. To ask them for money is to ask them, literally, for blood. Having lost the capacity to distinguish between money as necessity and money as luxury and power, they imagine that the loss of the third car or the second sailboat will cause them to vanish. When preoccupied with the existential question of their net worth, the expression in their eyes narrows into a lizard's stare.

LEWIS H. LAPHAM, *Money and Class in America*

Once, according to Kenneth Porter, when they stopped at a hotel on the Hudson for a cup of tea, John Jacob Astor pointed to the proprietor and said, "That man will never succeed."

"Why not?" asked his companion.

"Don't you see," said Astor in disgust, "what large lumps of sugar he puts in the sugar bowl?"

VIRGINIA COWLES, *The Astors*

On Halloween night in Washington, D.C., in the 1970s, children out for trick-or-treat stopped by the elegant N Street townhouse of Averell and Pamela Harriman. They were greeted by a maid in a white apron holding a silver tray full of dimes. How novel! The wealthy Harrimans—Pamela was the daughter of a British baron, Averell a financier and former Governor of New York—were handing out

they're stingy

money instead of candy. But not a lot. The maid cautioned: "Just one dime each."

Time magazine

[The Duke and Duchess of Windsor] believed, or so it appeared, that they should never be made to pay for anything, and they were to meet a number of Americans, in particular, prepared to think the same thing. Among them was a Pennsylvanian in the steel business who would be proud to foot the bill for complete restoration of the Duke's teeth.

MAVIS GALLANT, *Times Literary Supplement*

❖ HETTY GREEN, WHO had inherited several million dollars from her father which she parlayed into tens of millions in the stock market, nevertheless lived in flophouses, resold newspapers and empty bottles, and carried graham crackers in her purse in order to avoid the "prohibitive prices" of New York restaurants. When her son broke a leg in an accident, she delayed getting medical help for fear of the cost, at a time when her annual income was $7 million. She finally dressed the boy in rags to get free treatment at a charity ward. Unfortunately, the treatment was too late and the leg eventually had to be amputated.

❖ THE NIZAM OF HYDERABAD, a bona fide Oriental potentate believed to be the richest man in the world during the 1940s, was nonetheless a skinflint who wore tattered clothing and rolled his own cigarettes. Upon his death, his strong rooms were found to contain stacks of currency eaten through by rats, along with precious gems in color-coded safes—a red safe for rubies, a green one for emeralds, and a blue one for sapphires.

◈ WHEN AN EMPLOYEE mailed him a report fastened with a paper clip, the self-made American shipping tycoon Daniel K. Ludwig shot back a stern reprimand: "We don't pay to send ironmongery by mail." Ludwig applied the same thrift to his personal life, wearing the same ratty plastic raincoat for years.

◈ ARISTOTLE ONASSIS REFUSED to wear a coat at all: "Since I am known as a 'rich' person, I feel I have to tip at least five dollars each time I check my coat. On top of that, I would have to wear a very expensive coat, and it would have to be insured. Added up, without a topcoat I save over twenty thousand dollars a year."

◈ THE CANADIAN NEWSPAPER mogul and centimillionaire Roy Thomson always flew tourist class and carefully weighed his luggage beforehand to avoid overweight charges.

◈ NOT ONLY DID Sam Walton, the billionaire founder of Wal-Mart, always fly coach, he drove a broken-down old pickup truck. When asked why he didn't drive something more in keeping with his status as the richest man in the country, Walton replied, "Am I supposed to haul my dogs around in a Rolls-Royce?"

they're stingy

◈ THE LATE "Orange Juice King," Ben Hill Griffin, Jr., drove a Jeep Wagoneer with over 100,000 miles on it.

◈ THE RAILROAD BARON Russell Sage routinely haggled with fruit vendors over the price of apples at a time when his annual income was in the millions.

◈ THOUGH HE DONATED over $60 million to charity during his lifetime, Julius Rosenwald, the man who built Sears, Roebuck into a retail colossus, dressed his family in secondhand clothes.

◈ THE OIL BILLIONAIRE H. L. Hunt took his lunch to the office in a paper bag.

◈ THE OIL BILLIONAIRE J. Paul Getty washed his own undershorts every night.

◈ JOHN D. MACARTHUR, the founder of the multibillion-dollar foundation that awards "genius grants," had a genius for thrift. He carried his lunch in a paper bag, took doggy bags home from restaurants, and dressed in worn clothes. He lived in a dilapidated Palm Beach hotel where he conducted business from the coffee shop, and would send his son out to use a pay phone to avoid the hotel's 10-cent-per-call surcharge. When he died, his executor found several buckets on the floor of his bedroom placed to catch leaks from the roof.

◈ THE MEATPACKING MOGUL Gustavus Swift regularly inspected the sewers behind his Chicago plant for evidence of "wasted" fat.

◈ ROSE KENNEDY WAS a virtuoso of domestic economy. According to a former secretary, Mrs. Kennedy once ordered the cook not to fix a baked potato because of the cost of turning on the oven. She habitually returned used cosmetics to the local drugstore for credit, and as the matriarch of a large family, she always made sure each of her twenty-nine grandchildren got a check on his or her birthday. A check for fifteen dollars.

◈ WHEN THE REAL ESTATE mogul Harry Helmsley bought the New York Central Building in Manhattan, the contract required him to change the name, which was chiseled on the façade. Ever the thrifty millionaire, he changed "Central" to "General," so that only two letters would have to be replaced rather than a whole word. And when his stepson's coffin could not fit in his private jet, Helmsley reluctantly had it shipped on a commercial airliner, then sued the estate for reimbursement.

◈ THE MULTIBILLIONAIRE INVESTOR Warren Buffett, whose income has been estimated at $8 million a month, has simple tastes. He lives in the same house in Omaha, Nebraska, he bought in 1957 for $31,500. His wife once said of him: "All Warren needs to be happy is a book and a sixty-watt bulb."

they're stingy

The outward forms of piety sometimes seemed more important to Sara than their intrinsic meaning. Every Friday evening, clad in her best jewelry and most fetching hats, she presided like a sovereign over family dinners. The furniture, silver candlesticks, and glasses sparkled. The devout Sara wouldn't extinguish Sabbath candles. Instead, she put her pouting lips by the candles and recited a couplet that mentioned two Jewish holidays, Purim and Pesach. The hard "p" sounds blew the candles out, saving her from sin.

RON CHERNOW, *The Warburgs*

they're extravagant

◆ THE ECCENTRIC NEWSPAPER tycoon James Gordon Bennett once gave a $14,000 tip to a porter on a French train. The man immediately quit his job and opened a restaurant.

◆ AFTER A FIVE-DAY stay at the Four Seasons Hotel on Cyprus in 1993, the sultan of Brunei left a $170,000 tip for the staff along with a note that read: "A big thank you. . . . This is a small token of appreciation."

◆ THE SAUDI ARABIAN Oil Minister Sheik Ahmed Zaki al-Yamani once tipped a barber $300 for giving him a shave.

Whenever [Lord Lonsdale] moved from one house to another, a special train was reserved for his household. If he travelled overnight, one first-class sleeper was reserved for himself and another for his pack of foxhounds. Along the route station masters paraded on the platforms of their stations to see the Lonsdale train safely through, and to be rewarded with a five-pound note, handed out by Lonsdale's valet, who was required to stay up all night for the purpose.

DOUGLAS SUTHERLAND, *The Yellow Earl*

When Potter Palmer married Bertha Honoré, a beautiful young woman whose extravagance would prove equal to his considerable fortune, he gave her the Palmer House hotel in Chicago as a wedding gift. Once, after giving her a necklace containing seven diamonds and two hundred pearls, he stood back admiringly and said, "There she stands, with half a million on her back." And when he made a will leaving everything to Bertha, a lawyer pointed out that his money might fall into the hands of Bertha's potential second husband and suggested that Palmer put a provision in the will to prevent it. "No," Palmer replied, "He'll need it." Palmer died in 1902, and Bertha never remarried.

FROM THE TIME she became first lady of Argentina, Eva Perón boasted of never having worn any of her Dior dresses more than once.

All decent people live beyond their incomes nowadays, and those who aren't respectable live beyond other people's. A few gifted individuals manage to do both.

SAKI (H. H. MUNRO)

At lunch I listened to a lawyer who for some months had been disbursing funds for the work of interior reconstruction in a large apartment overlooking Central Park. His client, a woman distracted by her

The Rich Are Different

ambition to become acquainted with "the best people," had already spent nearly $2 million, at least half of which had been allocated to the marble surfacing of the walls and floors. On first being shown the effect of the foyer, the woman pronounced it too cheap, too insufficient, too exposed to the condescension of the guests whom she expected to astonish at dinner. They'll think I'm tacky," she had said. "They'll know I only spent $100,000 for the marble."

In order to make a bath and dressing room large enough to accommodate her self-esteem, her contractor had broken through three walls and joined what were once two bedrooms into a space that could bear decoration in the manner of Imperial Rome. Still the result was somehow too small. That morning she had instructed the architect to supply additional mirrors and to install an icebox in the wall next to the tub. "She needs the icebox to chill the cologne," the lawyer said. "She said that there's nothing so unpleasant as to step out of a bath on a warm day and have to wear tepid cologne."

LEWIS H. LAPHAM, *Money and Class in America*

they're extravagant

they gamble for high stakes

◆ DURING THE 1887 Saratoga racing season, William Collins Whitney lost $385,000 at the gambling tables while waiting for his wife to finish dressing.

◆ THE BARBED-WIRE promoter John Warne "Bet-a-Million" Gates won $600,000 in one race betting on his horse, Royal Flush. He was also reputed to have bet thousands of dollars on the progress of raindrops trickling down a train window. Gates played bridge at the Waldorf-Astoria for "ten a point"; once, when a newcomer sat down to play, he assumed it was ten cents. Only when the game was over and Gates paid him $33,000 did the man realize they'd been playing for ten *dollars* a point.

One when his private car, a well-known landmark of the era in the Southwest, was spotted at Kansas City, a local sport begged audience, saying that he represented a syndicate and might he have an opportunity of playing some game, any game, with Mr. Gates?

"You know I don't play for small sums," Gates warned him.
"How much have you got to spend?"

The emissary produced a bank of $40,000.

Gates spun a $20 gold piece in the air. "Heads or tails, you
call it."

The local sport lost, Gates pocketed the banknotes, and the
loser reported his Waterloo to the syndicate. He became something of
a local celebrity and drummers in the lobby of the Muehlbach Hotel
pointed him out as the man who had lost $40,000 to Bet-a-Million
Gates in less than ten seconds.

LUCIUS BEEBE, *The Big Spenders*

As a boy I occasionally watched my grandfather play bridge at the
Pacific Union Club in San Francisco. He played for large stakes, but
he thought it unsporting to look at his cards before making an open-
ing bid. He never had trouble rounding up a fourth, and for the last
twenty years of his life he lost—not only at bridge, but also at golf,
cribbage and piquet—roughly $5,000 a day. He lacked the courage to
resist the will to lose, and nothing pleased him so much as the chance
to dissolve himself in the acid baths of the polymorphous perverse,
striking simultaneously at both time past (the money inherited from
his father) and time future (the money he might otherwise have given
to his children).

LEWIS H. LAPHAM, *Money and Class in America*

The Schlock of the Nouveau

In order to gain and to hold the esteem of men it is not sufficient merely to possess wealth or power. The wealth or power must be put in evidence, for esteem is awarded only on evidence.

THORSTEIN VEBLEN, *The Theory of the Leisure Class*

We have no aristocracy of blood, and having therefore as a natural, and indeed as an inevitable thing, fashioned for ourselves an aristocracy of dollars, the *display of wealth* has here to take the place and perform the office of the heraldic display in monarchical countries. By a transition readily understood, and which might have been as readily forseen, we have brought to merge in simple *show* our notions of taste itself.

EDGAR ALLAN POE

The extravagance of our era's Kravises, Gutfreunds, and Basses pales beside that of the Renaissance merchant class—the bourgeoisie that emerged with the rise of European commerce in the fourteenth and fifteenth centuries and celebrated its burgeoning wealth so ostentatiously that an alarmed nobility enacted sumptuary laws to curb the flamboyant nobility.

HELEN CONSTANTINO FIORATTI

There's a lot to be said for being nouveau riche, and the Reagans mean to say it all.

GORE VIDAL

Art museums generally are more prestigious than cultural institutions like libraries, because books—most books, anyway—have some practical purpose, which means that as a whole they lack the wastefulness necessary for a pure act of conspicuous consumption. Also, art is more expensive than books, and thus provides a greater opportunity to sustain pecuniary damage. Between 1983 and 1989 the Met took in $10 million from Laurence Tisch, $10 million from Milton Petrie, and $10 million from Henry Kravis, to mention only three of the largest bequests. The ability to absorb such huge amounts of money helps explain why art museums are more prestigious than ballet or opera companies. Furthermore, a gift to produce a ballet or opera disappears as soon as the curtain comes down. A gift to the Met for an acquisition or even a gallery—hardly anyone gives to the operating budget—provides evidence of the donor's power and wealth for a long, long time.

JOHN TAYLOR, *Circus of Ambition*

❖ TO HYPE THE VALUE of his then mediocre art collection, Armand Hammer hired armed guards to accompany his paintings wherever they went.

The day of showing off wealth in the pages of a decorating magazine had not yet dawned [in the 1880s], so to flaunt it, you had to get people in. And that meant you had to buy a punch bowl. Punch was the most universal drink at parties—the equivalent of today's white wine—and the punch bowl, with its ladle and silver cups, was set in the place of honor. In an era when consumption could never be conspicuous enough, it was an ideal pretext to show just how rich you were.

OLIVIER BERNIER, *American Heritage*

❖ RUSSIA'S EMERGING COWBOY capitalist class has its own magazine, *Domovoi*, which advises them on how to handle their new money, including how to shop at Moscow's Versace store (don't compete for the merchandise with the store's "whiny customers," order the designs directly from Paris fashion shows) and how to talk to a maid: "Speak in a calm tone, but it should be clear that what you say is an order."

You see them everywhere, seated at the expensive cafés along the Danube, making deals in the lobby of the Atrium Hyatt, handing their Mercedes and BMWs to tuxedoed parking attendants. At night they go to places like the Nautilus Nightclub and Restaurant, which is made entirely out of fish tanks, where they have whiskey surrounded by tropical fish that swim under their feet and over their heads, and eat such things as blinis with caviar and octopus Provençale from gold plates. They pay with large denomination *deutsche marks* and speak English with the waiters, dipping into Hungarian only when it's absolutely necessary, like in the marble toilet where the attendant speaks only the vulgate.

    ANDREI CODRESCU, "The *Nouveaux Riches* of Hungary"

From Poland to polo in one generation.

    ANONYMOUS Hollywood wag's description of
    Darryl F. Zanuck

I am not rich. I am a poor man with money, which is not the same thing.

    GABRIEL GARCÍA MÁRQUEZ

they're philanthropists
(sort of)

Studies have shown that on average the very rich in the United States give away only a tiny percentage of their total wealth. And when they do make charitable contributions, they demand and receive much in return, including tax breaks, favorable publicity, influence on the institutions to which they contribute, and what they seem to consider a form of immortality.

Cui bono? (Who profits?)

CICERO

He who gives while he lives also knows where it goes.

PERCY ROSS

Socially prominent people are very fond of disease, because it gives them a chance to have these really elaborate charity functions, and the newspaper headlines say EVENING IN PARIS BALL RAISES MONEY TO FIGHT GOUT instead of RICH PEOPLE AMUSE THEMSELVES.

DAVE BARRY

People in our world are swimming in money but in order to get [New York City's] rich to give a lousy thousand dollars to the poor who are drowning in front of their eyes you have to . . . give them party favors.

FELIX ROHATYN

Viewing the matter in retrospect, I can testify that it is nearly always easier to make one million dollars honestly than to dispose of it wisely.

JULIUS ROSENWALD

Giving away a fortune is taking Christianity too far.

CHARLOTTE BINGHAM

◈ AFTER JOHN D. ROCKEFELLER'S advisors prescribed philanthropy as an antidote to a severe image problem, he initiated a strong family tradition of giving. From his estate of approximately $1 billion, he bequeathed $250 million to the Rockefeller Foundation, $130 million to the General Education Board, $60 million to Rockefeller University, and $45 million to the University of Chicago.

◈ _____

The minister of Jay Gould's church asked the railroad tycoon where he might invest his life savings of $30,000. Gould recommended the stock of the Missouri Pacific Railroad, and, sworn to secrecy, the minister followed his advice. When the stock's price lost most of its value, Gould reimbursed the minister for his losses, whereupon the contrite clergyman confessed to Gould that he had passed the tip along to several other members *of the congregation. "Oh, I assumed you would," Gould said. "They were the ones I was after."*

While visiting Ireland, Henry Ford, asked to contribute to an orphanage, promptly donated £2,000. His generosity was reported in the local newspaper, but the amount was erroneously quoted as £20,000. Before the paper could correct the mistake, Ford wrote out a check for the difference.

IN THE MID-1970s, the developer Saul Steinberg pledged $375,000 to Lawrence Woodmere Academy, his children's prep school, but failed to pay most of it on the grounds that the "severe and dire" condition of the state of Israel had caused him to reorder his philanthropic priorities. Woodmere sued for payment of the balance and won.

WHEN THE MILKEN FOUNDATION donated $5 million to a Jewish high school in Los Angeles in return for having the school renamed Milken Community High School, critics charged that it was inappropriate to name the school after Michael Milken, the "Junk Bond King" and convicted felon who had served twenty-two months in federal prison and paid a $600 million fine for securities fraud. The principal insisted that the school was not being named for an individual, but for an entire family, and that the Milken Foundation had previously made donations to such organizations as the University of California and the Catholic Archdiocese of Los Angeles without mishap. Dennis Prager, a local radio talk-show host and a prominent member of the Los Angeles Jewish community, agreed: "If one member of a philanthropic family does wrong," he said, "and if that invalidates the family name, then clearly the Kennedy Center, Stanford University and the Carnegie Foundation all should change their names." Meanwhile, back on campus, some students suggested that the school's sports nickname be changed from the Wildcats to the Milken Cookies.

When the twenty-five-year-old Charles Lindbergh flew solo from New York to Paris in 1927, the world hailed him as a hero and commercial aviation received a tremendous boost. It is less remembered that in 1919, a wealthy French hotelier named Raymond Orteig had offered a $25,000 prize to the first aviator to cross the Atlantic. Thus the flight of the "Lone Eagle" was fueled by a rich man's prize.

When J. P. Morgan was asked to contribute to the construction of a medical school, he said he was in a hurry but would have a quick look at the plans. "I'll give that, that, and that," he said, pointing to three different buildings on the blueprints, upon which he hurried out of the room.

◈ A TEXAS OIL millionaire named H. R. Cullen gave a cumulative total of $100 million to the University of Houston and then threw in an extra $2.5 million when the Houston football team beat its archrival, Baylor. Cullen also gave large sums to the Houston Symphony, which showed its gratitude by playing his favorite song, "Old Black Joe," whenever he was in the audience.

In 1939, upon learning that he had been awarded a $1,000 Rockefeller grant, a scornful Tennessee Williams wrote: "The very rich have such a touching faith in the efficacy of small sums."

they don't pay taxes

We don't pay taxes. Only the little people pay taxes.

LEONA HELMSLEY

◈ SOME WEALTHY AMERICANS have renounced their citizenship to avoid paying taxes. A loophole in the U.S. Tax Code exempts noncitizens from payment of capital gains and estate taxes. Although they deny that their decision had anything to do with taxes, among the prominent Americans identified in the press as having renounced their citizenship (whom critics have labeled "economic Benedict Arnolds") are Ted Arison, founder of Carnival Cruise Lines; John Dorrance III, a Campbell's Soup heir; Mark Mobius, an international money manager based in Hong Kong; Kenneth Dart, a billionaire foam cup maker who became a citizen of Belize and then got himself appointed special Belizian diplomatic envoy to Florida; and Michael Dingman, the chairman of a New England aerospace company who became a Bahamian citizen but claims it had nothing to do with taxes: "It's an honor to be a

Bahamian citizen. They have to want you. You can't buy your way in. This is not St. Kitts."

◈ WHEN ALL ELSE FAILS, the very rich lobby Congress for bespoke tax laws. Euphemistically called "transition rules" or "technical corrections" by legislators but more accurately dubbed "rifle shot" exemptions, these private tax provisions are tailored to specific individuals or corporations but are written cryptically to conceal who is being helped.

For example, the Tax Reform Act of 1968 excused the luxurious cruise ship SS *Monterey* from compliance with new provisions of the tax code. The law does not mention the *Monterey* by name, but states:

> *The amendments made by section 201 shall not apply to a 562-foot passenger cruise ship, which was purchased in 1980 for the purpose of returning the vessel to United States Service, the approximate cost of refurbishment of which is $47 million.*

The provision gave the ship's owners the investment tax credit and accelerated depreciation that the Tax Reform Act had eliminated for most other taxpayers, thereby saving them an estimated $8 million in taxes.

The 1986 law also granted an exemption to a wealthy Beverly Hills securities dealer named Bernard Gerald Cantor, while, again, disguising his identity in dense language:

Special Rules for Broker-Dealers—In the case of a broker-dealer which is part of an affiliated group which files a consolidated Federal income tax return, the common parent of which was incorporated in Nevada on January 27, 1972, the personal holding income (within the meaning of Section 543 of the Internal Revenue Code of 1986) of such broker-dealer, shall not include any interest received after the date of enactment of this Act. . . .

After billions of dollars worth of such loopholes were included in the Tax Reform Act of 1986, the practice was exposed in a series of articles by Donald L. Barlett and James B. Steele, investigative reporters for the *Philadelphia Inquirer:*

> When Congress passed the Tax Reform Act of 1986, radically overhauling the Internal Revenue Code, Rep. Dan Rostenkowski (D., Ill.), chairman of the tax writing House Ways and Means Committee, hailed the effort as "a bill that reaches deep into our national sense of justice—and gives us back a trust in government that has slipped away in the maze of tax preferences for the rich and powerful."
>
> In fact, Rostenkowski and other self-styled reformers created a new maze of unprecedented favoritism. Working in secret, they wove at least 650 exemptions—preferences, really, for the rich and

powerful—through the legislation, most written in cryptic legal and tax jargon that conceals the identity of the beneficiaries.

When they were finished, thousands of wealthy individuals and hundreds of businesses were absolved from paying billions upon billions of dollars in federal income taxes. It was . . . the largest tax giveaway in the 75-year history of the federal income tax. . . . Whatever the economic cost of personal tax breaks, it is dwarfed by the cost in fairness.

In 1986, Congress extended preferential treatment to thousands of individual taxpayers and hundreds of companies at the expense of other individuals and companies in similar situations.

It gave tax breaks to urban development projects in some cities and withheld them in others. It gave tax breaks to some trucking companies and withheld them from others. It gave tax breaks to some insurance companies and withheld them from others. It gave tax breaks to some housing projects and withheld them from others. It gave tax breaks to some utilities and withheld them from others. It gave tax breaks to some universities and withheld them from others. It gave tax breaks to some communications companies and withheld them from others. It gave tax breaks to the steel industry and withheld them from the copper industry.

Without exception, Congress denied comparable breaks to middle-income taxpayers who shoulder the brunt of the overall federal tax burden. But this was in keeping with the way Congress has been making tax law since the late 1960s.

The practice continues. Lobbyists still come before the House Ways and Means Committee for hearings on these private tax favors (now code-named "miscellaneous tax reforms"), and they are still being written into law.

◈ JACOB FREIDUS, A WEALTHY octogenarian from Cold Spring Harbor, New York, hasn't paid a penny of income tax since 1949, when, after amassing a $15-million real estate fortune, he was charged with federal income tax evasion and was sentenced to four years in prison. While serving his time Freidus hatched a tax avoidance scheme involving the transfer of assets to a dummy corporation, as a result of which the IRS billed him for $9 million in back taxes. But Freidus refused to pay, and so began *U.S. v. Jacob Freidus*, the longest-running case in the history of federal tax litigation. After three decades of delays and legal maneuvering, when penalties and interest had swelled the unpaid debt to $20 million (he also owes the state of New York $460,000) and he had exhausted all his appeals, Freidus declared bankruptcy.

they don't pay taxes

◈ IN A WELL-PUBLICIZED case of creative tax planning, while he occupied the White House, President George Bush avoided paying income tax in the District of Columbia on the ground that he was domiciled in Texas, his qualifying "home" being a Houston hotel room where he spent no more than a few nights a year.

◈ IN A HIGHLY VISIBLE example of a common practice among rich business owners, the late magazine publisher and bon vivant Malcolm Forbes turned his hobbies into tax deductions. He appropriated a pejorative term coined by Soviet cold-war propagandists and employed it as an ironic slogan for his magazine, emblazoning the words "Capitalist Tool" on everything from the tail of his 727 to the skin of a mammoth hot-air balloon. Such usage qualified as "advertising," hence the cost of the pricey toys became deductible business expenses.

Over and over again courts have said that there is nothing sinister in so arranging one's affairs as to keep taxes as low as possible. Everybody does so, rich and poor; and all do right, for nobody owes any public duty to pay more than the law demands: taxes are enforced exactions, not voluntary contributions. To demand more in the name of morals is mere cant.

LEARNED HAND

Anybody has a right to evade taxes if he can get away with it. No citizen has a moral obligation to assist in maintaining the government. If

Congress insists on making stupid mistakes and passing foolish tax laws, millionaires should not be condemned if they take advantage of them.

J. P. MORGAN

❖ IN 1989, LEONA HELMSLEY was sentenced to four years in prison for evading over $1 million in federal taxes. She had illegally charged a variety of personal expenses to Helmsley corporations, from a $1 million swimming pool enclosure on her Connecticut estate to a $12.99 girdle from Bloomingdale's. She served eighteen months and was assigned 750 hours of community service, but in June 1995 members of her domestic staff revealed that they had performed the court-ordered work for her.

Overwhelmingly, taxes collected from individual Americans are based on their annual income. (The income can come from paychecks, fees, dividends, or profits from sale of assets.) The policeman's income via paycheck may account for 95 percent of his wealth. In contrast, the billionaire's annual income may be less than 1 percent of his wealth. If he has expert estate planners, his income may be just enough to pay his bills. He may take no salary or only a nominal one. He may place his wealth in land (perhaps oil-rich land) or stocks with negligible yields, perhaps stock in his own company. Land and nondividend stocks simply grow and grow. There need be no federal tax reckoning whatsoever until he sells these assets or until he dies. And by death his lawyers have usually dispersed much or most of his taxable assets

they don't pay taxes

through trusts and other strategies. (His advisers may shun bonds because bonds pay income in the form of interest.)

Presently the U.S. government collects about sixty times as much from income taxes on the general populace as it does from the estate and gift taxes it imposes when huge assets are transferred by rich people to their heirs.

So a logical question arises: Since we are witnessing a great leap in accumulation of large fortunes at a time when real assets of the average person are declining, why do we not put a direct tax on wealth?

VANCE PACKARD, *The Ultra Rich*

The Windsors were legally residents of France. Unlike any other foreign resident, they were not required to pay income tax. The city of Paris . . . had made them an indefinite loan of a large house on the edge of the lovely Parc de Bagatelle, in the Bois de Boulogne. When the Duke died, no death duties were claimed—another astonishing dispensation—and the Duchess was allowed to remain in the house, on the same generous terms, until her own death in the mid-1980s.

MAVIS GALLANT, *Times Literary Supplement*

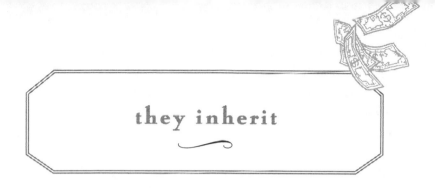

they inherit

What's the use of money if you have to earn it?

GEORGE BERNARD SHAW, *Man and Superman*

Saving is a very fine thing. Especially when your parents have done it for you.

WINSTON CHURCHILL

Widowhood is a fringe benefit of marriage.

CLARE BOOTHE LUCE

The large inheritance of wealth probably has the effect of reducing the incentives to the heir to exercise his full capabilities—he has received the gold medal at the beginning of the race.

GEORGE J. STIGLER

It's hard to pull yourself up by the bootstraps when you're wearing Top-Siders.

HOWARD OGDEN, *Pensamentoes*

At college I was struck by the way in which heirs to even modest fortunes fitted their lives into small spaces. They had the resources to travel extensively, to underwrite the acts of the imagination (their own or those of others), to make the acquaintance of their own minds. Instead, they fixed their attention on the tiny distinctions between shirts bought at Tripler's and shirts bought at J. Press, between the inflections of voices in Greenwich, Connecticut, and the inflections of voices twenty miles north in Armonk. Their preoccupations were those of department store clerks or the editors of *New York* magazine.

LEWIS H. LAPHAM, *Money and Class in America*

My financial inheritance is one of the realities I have with difficulty developed the serenity to accept. I have struggled to transform my guilty energy into the courage to discover and try to change the things that I can change, if only a little.

LAURA ROCKEFELLER, quoted in *The Ultra Rich* by Vance Packard

I was born into it and there was nothing I could do about it. It was there like air or food or any other element. The only question was what to do with it.

JOHN D. ROCKEFELLER, JR.

She was born with an entire silver dinner service in her mouth.

CLIVE JAMES of Grace Kelly

When you have told anyone you have left him a legacy, the only decent thing to do is die at once.

SAMUEL BUTLER

You can get very hungry while waiting, if your livelihood depends on someone's decease. . . . Death does not always listen to the promises and prayers of those who would inherit.

MOLIÈRE

Men forget more easily the death of their father than the loss of their patrimony.

NICCOLÒ MACHIAVELLI

My life was never destined to be quite happy. It was laid out along lines which I could foresee almost from my earliest childhood. It has left me with nothing to hope for, with nothing definite to seek or strive for. Inherited wealth is a real handicap to childhood. It is as certain as death to ambition, as cocaine is to morality.

WILLIAM K. VANDERBILT (grandson of the "Commodore")

[Earned] money is much more satisfying to me. I always quote the Billie Holiday song: "Mama may have, Papa may have, but God bless the child that's got his own."

GLORIA VANDERBILT

they inherit

79

they spoil
their children

A fortune is usually the greatest of misfortunes to children. It takes the muscles out of the limbs, the brain out of the head, and virtue out of the heart.

HENRY WARD BEECHER

Excess wealth is a fatal disincentive to a productive life. Just as a boat will shake itself to pieces in a calm rather than a high wind, a listless child is almost certainly to be unhappy.

JOHN TRAIN

Wealth does not corrupt nor does it ennoble. But wealth does govern the minds of privileged children, gives them a particular kind of identity they never lose, whether they grow up to be stockbrokers or communards, and whether they lead healthy or unstable lives.

ROBERT COLES

Henry Ford II had always been an industrial prince. With the possible exception of Nelson and David Rockefeller and Averell Harriman, no public figure was raised in such splendor. He grew up in a 60-room house in Grosse Pointe, son of a refined mother and a father who was a passionate art lover. As a little boy he rode in his own child-sized railroad, authentic in all but dimensions, with a coal-burning locomotive. Before he was 10 he had a small British sports car and could drive it around the 90-acre estate.

DAVID HALBERSTAM

◈ WILLIAM RANDOLPH HEARST, himself a Harvard dropout, discouraged his five sons from attending college. He once wrote that "a certain kind of good mind does resist education." Accordingly he offered his son William Jr. a $100,000-a-year job if he would quit the University of California at Berkeley. "You can read and write," he said. "If you stay there any longer you're wasting your time." William Jr. quit and took over as president of the Hearst Company.

Hearst repeated the pattern with his other four sons, naming George publisher of the *San Francisco Examiner* after he dropped out of college, and he gave the other boys jobs in the Hearst Empire when they made their father proud by leaving college early. But they were only big salaries and impressive titles: The sons were given no say in running the companies, which was left to professional managers. And in the case of William Jr., the $100,000 a

they spoil their children

81

year was reduced to $15,000 when the company was forced to cut back during the Depression.

◈ HENRY FORD II once recalled for an interviewer that his doting grandfather had allowed him to sit in the cashier's office at the Ford Motor Company and play with the money.

Poor Little Rich Kids

They are overshadowed by their progenitors, who made all the money in the first place. Their parents, many of whom were poor little rich kids themselves, lack essential parenting skills and tend to ignore them, hence they're brought up by nannies and tutors. They're hounded by paparazzi and stalked by fortune hunters. To protect them from kidnappers, they're under the constant watch of bodyguards. If they manage to form friendships, they never really know whether they're liked for themselves.

Their wealth blunts ambition; they can buy anything they want—almost anything they can imagine. Yet they're unhappy. Lacking a sense of purpose in life, they're prone to bizarre behavior to assuage the emotional insecurity and overcome the ennui.

Doris Duke

If George Bernard Shaw had known Doris Duke, he might have changed his famous statement about youth to ask why it is that money has to be wasted on the rich.

PETER COLLIER, *Washington Post*

In 1925, when she inherited some $300 million at the age of thirteen, she was dubbed "the richest girl in the world." Her father, James B. Duke, the founder of the American Tobacco Company, warned her that people would be interested in her only for her money and that she should never trust anyone. She seems to have followed the advice: twice divorced and childless, she once complained, "I wish I could go into a store and shop for things just as a girl."

Upon their divorce, her first husband, who called her "my frigid heiress," sued for a financial settlement but lost. Her second husband, the international playboy Porfirio Rubirosa, fared much better: he got $1 million in cash and a string of polo ponies. For her part Duke collected a string of famous lovers, including General George S. Patton, Errol Flynn, and the Hawaiian swimming champion Duke Kahanamoku.

Doris Duke was intensely private, with no truly close friends, and little contact with her few relatives. She led a bizarre, erratic existence: she had an intense passion for belly dancing, and gave her two pet camels the run of her Beverly Hills mansion. She vacillated between lavish spending and abject parsimony. She rolled her hair with toilet paper to save money on bobby pins, and tore the labels out of her Parisian designer dresses to avoid paying customs duty. She could spend hundreds of thousands of dollars on landscaping for her various houses, and routinely bought $4,000 bottles of wine, but she deducted the cost of broken glassware from servants' paychecks, whom she would reprimand for putting too much postage on letters.

Though Doris Duke had few friends, she could occasionally display a certain loyalty: she posted $5 million in bail for her friend and Honolulu neighbor, Imelda Marcos, when the former first lady of the Philippines was indicted on fraud and racketeering charges for embezzling more than $100 million from her country. Duke's lawyer, acting on her behalf, turned over to the court more than $5 million worth of Duke's municipal bonds, explaining that because the bond market fluctuates, "we're giving them several hundred thousand more so the government won't beef about it." Marcos publicly expressed her gratitude, calling Duke "my Statue of Liberty."

In 1988, Duke legally adopted Chandi Heffner, a thirty-five-year-old former belly dancer and Hare Krishna, because she believed Heffner was the reincarnation of her only daughter, who had died shortly after being born in 1940. For several years the two women were inseparable, traveling back and forth between Duke's various residences and making pilgrimages to India together. Duke bought her a $1.5 million ranch in Hawaii and put a $5 million bequest to Heffner in her will. Then, perhaps remembering her father's warnings, Duke began to suspect that Heffner was trying to poison her in order to come into the inheritance, and she disowned and disinherited her in 1991. After Duke's death at the age of eighty, having received none of the billion-dollar estate, Heffner challenged the will and eventually obtained a $65 million settlement from Bernard Lafferty, Duke's executor and former butler.

Doris Duke may even have been murdered for her money: an attending nurse claims that her physician, Dr. Charles F. Kivowitz, and Lafferty, a former hotel maitre d', conspired to give her a fatal overdose of morphine, and the cook testified that on the day she died he heard Lafferty say, "Mrs. Duke's going to die tonight" after receiving a mysterious package. Both Lafferty (who refers to Duke as "my second mother") and the doctor vehemently deny the allegations. The truth may never be known: no autopsy was performed, and the body was cremated within hours of death.

Duke changed her will several times during the last five years of her life, and the final version was signed in her hospital room and witnessed by Dr. Kivowitz and Lafferty, who had been seen on Rodeo Drive shopping sprees while Duke lay comatose a few miles away, using her platinum American Express Card to run up over $60,000 in charges. Lafferty claimed that the purchases at Neiman Marcus, Giorgio Armani, Gucci, and Louis Vuitton were authorized by his employer and that he spent the money "because I wanted to represent Miss Duke in appropriate attire, which I did not have, I needed to purchase additional clothing." Lafferty spent another $60,000 to install a spa in Duke's former home in New Jersey, and purchased two miniature ponies "to provide companionship" for Duke's pet camel.

Duke left most of her $1.2 billion estate for the creation of the Doris Duke Foundation, which would benefit the arts, the environment, medical research, and animal welfare, and could become one of the largest in the nation. The will also left $10 million each to the Metropolitan Museum of Art and Duke University, and $100,000 for the upkeep of two dogs.

Duke's relatives and former employees have challenged the will on the ground that Lafferty exerted undue influence on Duke. The will gives him $500,000 per year for life and names him executor of the estate and a trustee of the prospective Doris Duke Foundation, positions that would earn him an additional $5 million in fees.

When a Surrogate Court judge ordered the estate to stop payments to Lafferty and his legion of lawyers after an investigation revealed that Mrs. Duke's death was indeed hastened by a series of morphine doses, he had already received an $825,000 interest-free loan from his cotrustee, the U.S. Trust Company, and had incurred a $10 million legal tab on behalf of the estate.

J. Paul Getty III

When J. Paul Getty III was kidnapped in 1973, his billionaire grandfather initially refused to pay the $2.8 million ransom, relenting only after the kidnappers mailed him the boy's festering ear (Italian postal workers were on strike and the ear had been in the mail for three weeks).

Negotiations with the kidnappers were hampered by the suspicion that Paul III had engineered the crime himself to raise funds. Paul III, wounded by his parents' divorce and his father's neglect, had taken to increasingly outrageous behavior. If a teacher criticized him at school, he would stick two fingers down his throat and throw up onto his desk. He roared around the Vatican on his motorcycle and fell in with a louche, druggy crowd that hung out around Piazza Navona.

The young hostage's grandfather was remarkably unsympathetic. Getty Sr. spent $6 million on art at Christie's in a single morning at the same time he was refusing to contribute to Paul III's ransom. "I don't believe in paying kidnappers," he announced in a brief statement. "I have 14 other grandchildren and if I pay one penny now, then I will have 14 kidnapped grandchildren.". . .

After his release, Paul III fell apart. Within months he wedded a German actress eight years his senior, though he knew that his grandfather would cut off any heir who married while still a teenager. Then, in 1981, he took a near-lethal cocktail of prescribed drugs that included Placidyl, Valium, Dalmane, and methadone, and suffered a massive stroke. To this day he lives completely paralyzed and almost completely blind, imprisoned in his still-alert mind.

FIAMMETTA ROCCO

Barbara Hutton

Another "richest girl in the world," she inherited $20 million from her grandfather, Frank Woolworth, when she turned twenty-one in 1930. She married a succession of foreign playboys: "Prince" Alexis Mdivani, Count Kurt von Haugwitz-Reventlow, Prince Igor Troubetzkoy, Porfirio Rubirosa, Baron von Cramm, and Prince Doan Vinh. Cary Grant, her third husband, refused to take any of her money when they parted (the press dubbed them "Cash and Cary").

Nothing infuriates me more than rich people saying they're unhappy because they have wealth. I always tell them they should go down on their knees and thank God they have money.

BARBARA HUTTON

Tommy Manville

Heir to the Johns-Manville insulation fortune, his trust fund guaranteed him $250,000 when he married. He married thirteen times. According to John Train, "He'd pay the woman $50,000, pocket $200,000, get a quickie divorce and then, when he needed more money, he'd get married again." Getting married would be his only claim to fame. He did it for the first time in 1911, at the age of seventeen, and went on to marry a succession of "actresses" and showgirls (*Newsweek* dubbed him "the Patron Saint of Chorus Girls"). He married his fifth wife, a twenty-two-year-old dancer, after a four-day engagement. "We're glad we waited to be sure," he explained. The marriage lasted two months. But the seventh marriage was the briefest: they were separated after eight hours (though the divorce didn't take effect for two months). By the time he died at the age of seventy-three, most of his fortune had been depleted by multiple alimonies. What remained went to the last Mrs. Manville, a waitress he had married in 1960 when he was sixty-six and she was twenty-two. He left no children.

The first thing I say to a girl is "Will you marry me?" The second thing is, "How do you do?"

TOMMY MANVILLE

Christina Onassis

The daughter of Greek shipping tycoon Aristotle Onassis, she was the quintessential poor little rich girl: her father ignored her emotionally while showering her with possessions (she was widely rumored to have dressed her dolls in Dior originals), and upon the death of his son, Alexander, Onassis is alleged to have asked, "Why couldn't it have been my daughter rather than my son?" She inherited the Onassis fortune after his death in 1975, including an annual income estimated at $50 million, but she was so emotionally needy that she had to hire friends, paying them by the week to be houseguests, though she imposed strange rules: no one was allowed to retire for the evening before she did, and absolutely no sex was permitted under her roof (the edict was strictly enforced: she instructed maids to check guests' sheets for evidence of lovemaking). She also paid a dissolute Argentine polo player $360,000 a year, plus expenses, to be her "personal companion."

She had a passion for Diet Coke, reputedly consuming up to twenty-four bottles a day. When she found herself in a country where it was unavailable, she would send her private jet for a supply, but never more than one hundred bottles at a time. When asked why only a hundred bottles, her housekeeper replied, "Because Madame did not want *old* Diet Coke." The cost worked out to approximately $300 a bottle. Ms. Onassis's palate became so sensitive that she could tell which bottling plant a given specimen had come from.

She had four husbands, including Sergei Kauzov, an alleged KGB agent with a gold front tooth, and the last one, Thierry Roussel, a pharmaceutical heir and the father of her only child, Athina. When Christina begged him to father another child with her after their divorce, Roussel obliged with a supply of his sperm, in exchange for a Ferrari Testarossa. He received more than $70 million upon her death of a heart attack in 1988 at the age of thirty-seven, presumably as the result of years of yo-yo dieting and prescription drug abuse.

It was with considerable distaste that we read the review of the biography of Christina Onassis. What a pathetically wasted life! With all of her millions, she did absolutely no good for anyone—especially herself. Where were the foundations, the good works, attempts to help the poor, hungry and homeless of the world? No, for her it was a tour of the road of self-indulgence. Obsessive sex, consoling herself with $300 bottles of Diet Pepsi and all the rest.

MR. & MRS. R. L. BROWN, letter to the *Chicago Tribune*

Lisa Marie Presley

The only child of Elvis Presley stands to inherit $150 million when she turns thirty. After seeing her father dead on the bathroom floor when she was nine years old, she led an isolated, lonely childhood, went through rehabilitation for drug and alcohol addiction, and after a failed first marriage she wed Michael Jackson in 1994 and became a Scientologist. Though the couple repeatedly denied allegations that the marriage was a two-pronged publicity stunt to divert attention from child molestation charges against Mr. Jackson and to launch Ms. Presley's singing career, she filed for divorce less than two years later, citing "irreconcilable differences."

Prince Albert Maria Lamoral Miguel Johannes Gabriel von Thurn und Taxis

Heir to one of Germany's oldest fortunes, estimated to be as high as $3 billion, Prince Albert is the son of the late Prince Johannes von Thurn und Taxis, a flamboyant playboy and avowed homosexual known as "Johnny TNT," who married a German countess at the age of fifty-four for the sole purpose of producing an heir. He died in 1990 at the age of sixty-four after an unsuccessful second heart transplant.

Prince Albert lives in a five-hundred-room Bavarian palace with his mother and two sisters, where he is attended by a staff of seventy-five servants who address him as "Your Highness." His inheritance includes six castles complete with art and porcelain treasures, forests and farmland in Europe, real estate in North and South

America, a bank, a brewery, and one of the world's great stamp collections. He is chauffeured about in a bulletproof Mercedes in the constant company of bodyguards. He once came home from school wanting to know why a schoolmate didn't have a Rembrandt, too.

Lance Reventlow

Reventlow was the only child of Barbara Hutton and a Danish count (the second of her seven husbands) both of whom were too busy globe-trotting to pay much attention to their son, who was raised by governesses. When he turned twenty-one in 1957, he inherited $8 million, some of which he spent to build a house in Hollywood with a swimming pool in the living room. (The revelry was so enthusiastic that the place was known as "Camp Climax.")

He was married three times, first to the actress Jill St. John, who divorced him after three years of marriage claiming that his passion for car racing left no room for her in his life. He was killed in a plane crash in 1972 at the age of thirty-six.

So you were born with brown eyes. I was born with money. It just makes life more convenient.

LANCE REVENTLOW

Athina Roussel

Athina, born in 1985, is the daughter of Christina Onassis (thus a second-generation poor little rich girl) and pharmaceutical heir Thierry Roussel. Her mother, who died three years after she was born, is reported to have ordered her carried by servants long after the child had learned to walk. She stands to inherit $2 billion when she reaches age eighteen. In the meantime, her annual allowance is over $4.5 million.

Gloria Vanderbilt

This great-great granddaughter of Cornelius Vanderbilt was, in 1934, at the age of ten, the object of a sensational custody fight between her emotionally distant mother, Gloria Morgan Vanderbilt, and her aunt, Gertrude Vanderbilt Whitney, and grandmother, Laura Kilpatrick Morgan, who eventually won the suit and reared her, along with a beloved governess whom Gloria called "Big Dodo Elephant." Gloria's father, Reginald Claypoole Vanderbilt, died of cirrhosis of the liver when she was an infant after having dissipated himself and his $25 million inheritance.

"Little Gloria's" childhood was marred by the notoriety of the custody suit. She was hounded by the press, and was asked to leave the exclusive Miss Porter's School because of all the "disrupting" publicity. After inheriting $4 million when she turned twenty-one, she had a succession of careers, as actress, playwright, novelist, painter, and businesswoman who has lent her name to everything from jeans to frozen yogurt.

She's been married four times: at seventeen she eloped with a Hollywood press agent named Pat De Cicco; she then married the conductor Leopold Stokowski (whom she fought for custody of their two sons); the film director Sidney Lumet; and the writer Wyatt Cooper, who died in 1978 after fifteen years of marriage. In 1988 she witnessed her son's suicide, and in 1995 she was forced to sell both her Manhattan townhouse and her Long Island estate to pay back taxes.

they have
adorable nicknames

From a list of
first names that
have appeared
in the *Philadelphia
Inquirer*'s society
column, compiled
in the *Philadelphia
Daily News*
by columnist
Stu Bykofsky
and reprinted
in *Harper's*,
May 1995.

Barkie	Minky
Bunky	Peppi
Bunty	Perky
Cackie	Phippy
Caughie	Pixie
Choppy	Pooh
Diny	Sibby
Dodo	Siggie
Dudy	Taddi
Elfie	Tenny
Floss	Trophy
Frolic	Weezie
Gee	Wiggie
Happy	Winky
Kinnie	Wistie
Marby	Woosie
Mesie	

they have titles

> FINANCIAL NECESSITY FORCES ME TO OFFER
> **BRITISH LORDSHIP FOR QUICK SALE**
> AT A PRICE OF £9,400 OR NEAREST OFFER. EXCELLENT
> LINEAGE, WELL-RESPECTED TITLE WITH NO DEBTS ATTACHED.
> FULL DOCUMENTATION INCLUDED IN SALE. CAN BE HELD BY
> AN INDIVIDUAL OF ANY RACE. ALLOWS YOU TO LEGALLY USE
> "LORD" IN YOUR NAME AND IS FULLY INHERITABLE.
> *Weekly Telegraph* (London)

British titles have long been for sale, if not quite so publicly:

As prime minister of a coalition, with no official party endorsement, Lloyd George needed money with which to fight the general elections of 1918 and 1922. The Conservative fund was exclusively for the use of the party, and the official Liberal funds were jealously guarded by the Asquithians. Accordingly, Lloyd George resolved to create his own personal campaign fund—ultimately amounting to more than £2 million—largely by the sale of honours to those "hardnosed men" who had done well out of the war, and who wished to establish themselves socially in the peace. There was even a recognized tariff: £10,000 for a knighthood, £30,000 for a baronetcy, and £50,000 upwards for a peerage.

. . . In the famous list of July 1922 . . . four of the five peerages awarded were, at best, dubious. One went to Sir William Vestey, who had ostensibly rendered great service to his country in war by placing his cold storage depots at the disposal of the government free of charge. In fact, the company had been paid, he had moved his meat business to Argentina to avoid paying British taxes, and English people had thus been put out of work. Another new peer, Sir Samuel Waring, was accused of having made a fortune out of wartime contracts for military equipment, yet also of having abandoned those shareholders who had lost money by investing in an earlier and unsuccessful company of his. A third, Sir Archibald Williamson, was widely thought to have traded with the enemy during the First World War. And Sir Joseph Robinson was a "Randlord," had already purchased a baronetcy in 1908, and was a publicly convicted swindler whose appeal had been dismissed by the Judicial Committee of the Privy Council as recently as November 1921. The only name beyond reproach was that of Sir Robert Borwick, who was merely a manufacturer of baking-custard powder.

DAVID CANNADINE, *The Decline and Fall of the British Aristocracy*

HOSTESS: It's a great secret, but I must tell you. My husband has been offered a peerage.

GUEST: Really! That's rather interesting. We thought of having one, but they're so expensive, and we are economising just now.

Punch cartoon, July 1922

"This fellow raises the grapes. He's got thousands of acres of them."

"What's his name?" asked Brett. "Veuve Cliquot?"

"No," said the count. "Mumms. He's a baron."

"Isn't it wonderful," said Brett. "We all have titles. Why haven't you a title, Jake?"

"I assure you, sir," the count put his hand on my arm. "It never does a man any good. Most of the time it costs you money."

"Oh, I don't know. It's damned useful sometimes," Brett said.

"I've never known it to do me any good."

"You haven't used it properly. I've had hell's own amount of credit on mine."

ERNEST HEMINGWAY, *The Sun Also Rises*

❧ *Belcourt,* Oliver Hazard Perry Belmont's sixty-room Newport palace cum stable. Belmont's pampered thoroughbreds occupied the ground floor and he lived upstairs. The steeds and their owner slept on fine Irish linen.

❧ *Biltmore,* George Washington Vanderbilt III's home in Asheville, North Carolina. Set on 130,000 acres, with exquisitely landscaped formal gardens and thousands of acres of trees, Biltmore employed more foresters than the U.S. Department of Agriculture. With 250 rooms, it is the largest private residence in America, but like many of the great houses of a bygone era, taxes and prohibitive maintenance costs have reduced it to a tourist attraction.

❧ *The Breakers,* Cornelius Vanderbilt II's Northern Italian Renaissance "cottage" in Newport, designed by Richard Morris Hunt, cost $5 million to build in 1895. As electric lighting had only recently been invented, the house was equipped with both electric and gas lamps. In its heyday over half of its seventy rooms were occupied by servants. Over the library mantelpiece was the motto: "Little do I care for riches." The Breakers is now the biggest tourist attraction in the state of Rhode Island.

◈ *Californie*, the Russian Prince Cherkassy's villa in Cannes where he employed fifty gardeners to change the flower beds every night so that he could gaze upon fresh blossoms every morning.

◈ *Château-sur-Mer*, the Richard Morris Hunt–designed Newport home of the Wetmores, whose fortune derived from the china trade. Hence the walk-in china closet housing a 3,500-piece collection with its own full-time curator.

◈ *Château de L'Horizon*, Aly Khan's villa on the French Riviera, where guests could slide down a water chute directly into the Mediterranean. The house had fabulous ocean views from every room, and an artificial moon for dark nights.

◈ *The Creeks*, Revlon CEO Ron Perelman's East Hampton estate, formerly owned by the late artist Alfonso Ossorio.

Perelman was told that the highest offer for the Creeks had been $9 million, so he quickly had his lawyer offer $10 million. The representative for Ossorio's estate said $10 million was too low. "But he said," recalls Perelman, "'If you really want to do a deal, I'll tell you what we can trade at today.'" In less than an hour, a price of $12 million was agreed upon and a deal was done.

The next morning, Perelman was back at the Creeks with architect Peter Marino to talk about renovations. Perelman wanted to move in by the July Fourth weekend, without fail. On the morning of Memorial Day, dozens of workers swarmed onto the property and started gutting the house. When Perelman arrived for July Fourth, the Creeks was ready. Every wall, every floor, every bathroom, every wire, every pipe, and every vent was new. The outside was re-stuccoed in the original sandstone color, and the red, white, and blue trim was now white. The house was fully air-conditioned, and the windows and staircases that Ossorio had closed off were open again. The original interior design of the house had been completely restored. It had all taken three weeks from the closing.

CRAIG HOROWITZ, *New York* magazine

❖ *Crossways*, Mrs. Stuyvesant Fish's Newport villa, where the highlight of her dinner parties was the gold table service for three hundred.

❖ *Deerlands*, the C. V. Whitneys' 55,000-acre "camp" on Tupper Lake in the Adirondacks. To insure privacy, the Whitneys installed a net across the lake to keep boats from coming near the house.

❖ *Dunellen Hall*, Harry and Leona Helmsley's twenty-eight-room mansion on twenty-six acres in Greenwich, Connecticut. The New

York real estate couple ran afoul of the IRS by illegally charging various home improvements to their commercial properties as business expenses, including an outdoor stereo system with speakers concealed in the shrubbery for $140,000, and a $1 million marble enclosure for one of the swimming pools.

❖ *Fair Lane*, Henry Ford's Dearborn, Michigan, estate on 1,300 acres, was completed in 1915 at a cost of $2.5 million, ten times the original budget. The sixty-room mansion had a twenty-four-foot-long banister carved from a single oak tree and walls covered with African rose leaf mahogany. Ford had a six-story powerhouse erected on the property which provided Fair Lane's electricity, with enough left over for 2,000 of his neighbors. During the labor strife of the 1930s, the house was fortified with machine-gun emplacements.

❖ *Ferrières*, the Rothschilds' 10,000-acre estate near Paris where one of the servants did nothing but prepare salads.

❖ *Halton House*, Alfred de Rothschild's English country estate where departing guests received hundred-count bundles of his famous "guinea panatellas," cigars which, if available today, would cost perhaps $50 apiece.

❖ *Hammersmith Farm*, the hundred-acre Auchincloss estate in Newport overlooking Narragansett Bay where a young Jacqueline Bouvier spent her summers, and which served as the "summer White

House" during the Kennedy Administration (and later as the backdrop for the movie version of *The Great Gatsby*.) It is now a Kennedy museum and is ranked the most desirable venue for a wedding reception by the magazine *Tried and Trousseau.*

◈ *Kykuit,* John D. Rockefeller's 4,000-acre estate on the Hudson River, with a classically inspired, forty-room Georgian mansion and formal gardens featuring a full-scale replica of the Medici Temple of Venus in Florence, complemented by stalactites and stalagmites imported from Italian caves.

◈ *Las Incas,* Mrs. Stephen "Laddie" Sanford's oceanfront Palm Beach villa with one room decorated entirely with seashells.

◈ *Lyndhurst,* Jay Gould's five-hundred-acre Irvington-on-Hudson estate where the railroad baron supervised the cultivation of thousands of orchids in a vast complex of greenhouses.

◈ *Mar-a-Lago,* Marjorie Merriwether Post's (and then-husband E. F. Hutton's) 65,000-square-foot, 115-room pink stucco palacio on eighteen acres, including a nine-hole golf course. (Post's other residences were *The Boulders* in Greenwich, Connecticut; *Carnegie Hill* in Manhattan; *Foxhall Road* and *Tregaron* in Washington, D.C.; *Hogarcito* in Palm Beach; *Hillwood* on Long Island and *Rosewall* in Pittsburgh.)

Mar-a-Lago is situated in Palm Beach between the Atlantic Ocean and Lake Worth, hence its name, Spanish for "from sea to lake." It was designed by Joseph Urban in 1924 and took some three hundred craftsmen four years to complete at a cost of $2.5 million. Construction of the gilded ceilings exhausted the nation's supply of gold leaf and work had to be halted until a fresh supply could be imported from Europe. The roof consists of 36,000 antique Spanish tiles, many dating back to the sixteenth century. The 2,000-square-foot kitchen has a floor-to-ceiling vault for the silver.

When Post died in 1973, the property went to the United States for use as a winter White House, but the government gave it back to the Post Foundation in 1980 because of the high upkeep. Donald and Ivana Trump bought it in 1985 for $10 million, and after their divorce they occupied it alternately under a joint custody agreement.

In 1995, after adding a 25,000-square-foot spa and a 900-foot-long security wall at a (Trump-estimated) cost of $15 million, the beleaguered former billionaire began renting out some of the spare rooms, and he announced the creation of an exclusive club with an initiation fee of $100,000 and annual dues of $3,000. After reportedly bestowing honorary memberships on Prince Charles and Henry Kissinger, Trump pronounced Mar-a-Lago "number one among the three great houses of America" (the other two being *San Simeon* in California and *The Breakers* in Newport) and claimed a preservationist motive for starting the club: "I own one hundred percent of Mar-a-Lago. It's my house and I live in a certain section of it. That won't change. But it costs three million dollars a year to maintain. This way, if I'm no longer around and there is nobody else to take my place to preserve Mar-a-Lago, it will be automatically sustained by the club."

Inside [Mar-a-Lago], at the mansion's center, a thirty-four-foot-high living room had been designed around a series of tall silk needlework tapestries which once hung in a Venetian palace. To sustain this Italian theme, the ceiling was hand-gilded in a sunburst design modified from the "thousand-winged ceiling" motif of the Accadèmia in Venice. Marjorie disliked ecclesiastical themes, so gold sunburst patterns were substituted for the angel faces of the original Accadèmia ceilings. Similarly, the seven arches surrounding the living room were decorated in a millefleur background with armorial insignia of Venetian dogs in lieu of those monks of the Accadèmia. Beneath this design hung rare gilded Spanish lanterns.

At the back of the living room, which was carpeted with a sixteenth-century Spanish rug, was a hooded Italian Gothic fireplace. Just beyond it one arch led to a small room called the "monkey loggia," which contained whimsical stone carvings of those creatures. Through a triple arch at the front of the living room was another small room, entered by way of four marble steps flanked by northern Italian Romanesque columns mounted upon stone lions. Within this tiny chamber were frescoes copied from the Riccardo Medici palazzo in Florence. Beyond it was the immense plate-glass window, said to be the largest ever made in North America, with its view of the Atlantic.

NANCY RUBIN, *American Empress: The Life and Times of Marjorie Merriwether Post*

◆ *Marble House* in Newport, built of African marble and furnished, down to its gold-paneled ballroom, by William K. Vanderbilt and his wife, Alva, at a cost of $11 million in 1891. Alva would later become the first American *grande dame* to get a divorce, after which she used Marble House as a meeting place for suffragettes.

◆ *Meadow Brook Hall,* built on 1,400 acres near Detroit in 1930 by Matilda Dodge, widow of the automobile manufacturer John Dodge. The 80,000-square-foot house had a hundred rooms, including a 2,400-square-foot great hall where the Tommy Dorsey band played at parties.

◆ *San Simeon,* William Randolph Hearst's 240,000-acre central California estate, including fifty miles of oceanfront and a private zoo, cost the media mogul an estimated $30 million to build and maintain. Its formal name was La Cuesta Encantada, the Enchanted Hill, but it was commonly known as Hearst's Castle. Hearst himself called it simply "the ranch."

The four-story, 74,000-square-foot main house, La Casa Grande, has thirty-seven bedrooms, forty-one bathrooms, and so many levels that Hearst had to issue maps to befuddled guests, whom he would astonish by making miraculous entrances through the use of secret elevators.

There were twenty-four full-time gardeners to maintain the seven miles of hedges and the hundreds of imported Spanish fan palm and Italian cypress trees. When Hearst decided that the sight of a 1.2-million-gallon reservoir offended him, he had 6,000 pine trees planted to hide it.

Hearst had a penchant for European bric-a-brac. He had an entire Spanish monastery dismantled, shipped over, and reconstructed at the seaside castle. In a bit of studied eccentricity, he decreed that ketchup bottles be placed on the dining tables.

Now owned by the state, San Simeon is California's second most popular tourist attraction, after Disneyland.

It was sort of eerie. From the moment you stepped into the car . . . until you were returned to your own front door, you were the guest of Mr. Hearst. You didn't have to bring your wallet; there was nothing to spend money on. If you weren't driven to San Simeon, you made the journey either in Mr. Hearst's plane—very dashing in those days—or in a private railroad car. Either way, you were finally driven up the hillside into another world and another time.

The first time I saw the "castle," it seemed unreal, strangely forbidding and frightening at the crown of the yellow foothills. The road up the hill to the castle went through a series of giant corrals, each fenced and gated and each containing all manner of wild animals. A private jungle-cum-zoo. No stopping or getting out. As each gate closed behind you, you felt more and more as if you were being swallowed up, that time was running backwards and you might never be seen again.

SLIM KEITH, Slim: Memories of a Rich and Imperfect Life

The huge, glowing indoor pool at San Simeon—where people swam in winter, and met at night—has the stars and planets paved in blue-and-gold mosaic on its bottom. They are magnified and illuminated, these heavenly bodies, so they seem not settled under the water but rather floating on its surface. Above, on the ceiling of the pool house, is a representation of the ocean floor: fish and seaweed and shells.

"It's an upside-down world," a tour guide says, her voice echoing gently off the far wall. "And when you stand at the end of the diving board and look down, you are diving into the night sky."

MARTHA SHERRILL, Vanity Fair

◈ *Shangri-La*, Doris Duke's Indo-Persian palace near Honolulu. She had an entire coconut grove transplanted because she was too impatient for the trees to grow. Her bedroom had a stream running through it, and there were sumptuous bathrooms with jade fixtures, a dining room with aquarium walls, an aviary, a lily pond, and a working soda fountain.

❧ *Sky Farm*, W. W. Crocker's Hillsborough, California, estate, where among the forty in staff, one maid's full-time job was polishing the silver.

❧ *Stan Hywet Hall*, an eighty-room Tudor Revival mansion on 3,000 acres near Akron, Ohio, was the home of Frank Seiberling, founder of the Goodyear Tire and Rubber Company. The house was completed in 1915 at a cost of $3 million. During construction Mrs. Seiberling ordered workmen to cut scuff marks in the floor to give them a "lived-in" look.

❧ *Sutton Place*, J. Paul Getty's estate near London (formerly the home of the Duke of Sutherland) with a private trout stream, various lodges and cottages, and a seventy-two-room main house containing Getty's fabulous art collection and a notorious pay phone: "The guests won't mind paying for their calls," he explained, "and as for the deadbeats, I couldn't care less."

I remember once, when we were staying with Paul Getty at Sutton Place, I said, "Paul, I'm shivering." There were fireplaces everywhere, but none of them lit. He shrugged, "We have no wood." He was too stingy to buy any!

ROSEMARIE KANZLER, *W*

their houses have names

◈ *Versailles Palace*, arguably the most ostentatious residence ever built, was begun in 1661 by King Louis XIV as a hunting lodge. His two immediate successors added to it so that by Louis XVI's reign it was a half mile long with hundreds of rooms, including its own grottoes, temples, and opera house.

Built at an estimated cumulative cost of some $200 million, its construction and upkeep helped bankrupt the French monarchy, fanning the outrage of the French people, which culminated in the Revolution of 1789, when the palace was ransacked by angry mobs. It has since been rebuilt, and now serves as a museum and major tourist attraction.

The French Revolution was a palace revolt—and the revolting palace was Versailles.

M. HIRSH GOLDBERG, *The Complete Book of Greed*

◈ *Waddeston*, the nineteenth-century home of Alfred Rothschild, where a famous exchange is supposed to have occurred:

BUTLER: Tea or coffee, sir?
GUEST: Tea, please.
BUTLER: China, India, or Ceylon, sir?
GUEST: China, please.
BUTLER: Lemon, milk, or cream, sir?
GUEST: Milk, please.
BUTLER: Jersey, Hereford, or Shorthorn, sir? . . .

◈ *Whitemarsh Hall,* Ned and Eva Stotesbury's suburban Philadelphia mansion, with forty-five bedrooms, a tailor shop, and a 300-acre garden, where each guest was assigned a personal car and chauffeur. After a visit Henry Ford remarked that he found it interesting to see how the rich live.

◈ *Wintoon,* William Randolph Hearst's San Francisco estate on which he built a replica of a Bavarian village. Hearst liked to roam the property dressed in Tyrolean garb arm in arm with Marion Davies, who dubbed it "Spittoon."

◈ *Wormsley,* J. Paul Getty, Jr.'s 2,500-acre estate in Buckinghamshire where Getty's own cricket team plays on its own ground. Getty's $75-million collection of rare books and manuscripts is housed in a library the ceiling of which is painted with the pattern of the heavens as they appeared on the night Getty was born.

In her lifetime it had been Mrs. Whitelaw Reid's occasional and usually whimsical boast that at no time when traveling abroad or in the United States was it necessary for her to sleep under a roof that wasn't her own. In New York City there was the Villard mansion on Madison Avenue, and, at White Plains, *Ophir Hall* and *Ophir Hall's* suburb, *Ophir Cottage,* a forty-room villa next door occupied by her son and daughter-in-law. There was *Millbrae* in Burlingame when she was in California, a camp at Paul Smith's in the Adirondacks, and *Flyaway,* a hunting lodge on Currituck Sound in North Carolina. There was a town house in Paris and during the term of Whitelaw Reid's embassy to St. James's a mansion at Carlton House Terrace in London. When Mrs. Reid died in 1931 it was under the roof of the Cap Ferrat villa of her daughter, Lady John Ward.

LUCIUS BEEBE, *The Big Spenders*

they live in fabulous houses

In the early 1920s, soon after the prominent corporation lawyer Paul D. Cravath had built a lavish estate on Long Island at a cost of $300,000, he decided something was missing and inquired of the architect whether a running brook might be installed in the drawing room. The unflappable architect replied, "What kind of brook do you want? One that burbles or babbles?" "Both," said Cravath. The bill came to $75,000.

THE TELEVISION PRODUCER Aaron Spelling's 120-room, 55,000-square-foot faux French château on five acres in Holmby Hills (near the Los Angeles Country Club and the Playboy Mansion) took four years and $50 million to complete. It is built on the site of Bing Crosby's former home, itself a 20,000-square-foot mansion, which Spelling, the producer of *The Love Boat*, *Dynasty*, and *Beverly Hills 90210*, bought in 1983 for $10.5 million (in L. A. real estate parlance, a "tear-down"). The Spelling mansion has four two-car garages, a bowling alley, a fifty-seat screening room, and a windowless strong room with an independent air supply and steel walls in case of terrorist attack. The dressing rooms are so vast and well-stocked that their shelves are accessed by a system of catwalks. The neighbors refer to the four-story building as "the Holmby Hyatt."

◈ BARBRA STREISAND'S MALIBU HOUSE was furnished in authentic 1920s art nouveau, down to the period cars in the garage, color-coordinated with the interior of the house.

◈ THE THREE-STORY, 15,000-square-foot Kirkeby mansion in Bel Air was built for Guy Atkinson, whose company had built Boulder Dam, and was sold to the millionaire developer Arnold Kirkeby after Atkinson committed suicide. In 1962 the television pro-ducer Paul Henning persuaded the Kirkebys to let him use the house in his new sitcom about a family of hillbillies from Okla-homa who strike it rich and move to Beverly Hills. Unfortunately for the neighbors, *TV Guide* revealed the location of the house and it's been a tourist attraction ever since, with a steady stream of sightseers in cars and buses driving by, stopping for photographs, and generally disrupting the otherwise exclusive neighborhood.

◈ JOSEPH PULITZER'S FIFTH AVENUE mansion was soundproofed with $2 million worth of extra marble.

❖ IN 1978, SHEIK MOHAMMED AL-FASSI, a cousin by marriage to King Fahd of Saudi Arabia, paid $2.4 million for an old Beverly Hills mansion on 3.5 acres and immediately began to remodel. He had the roof gilded, had thousands of plastic flowers planted, had the stucco painted a sickly green (described by one neighbor as "the color of rotting limes") and had the genitalia and pubic hair on the garden statuary painted bright red and black respectively.

The house became a tourist attraction, causing traffic jams on Sunset Boulevard. Outraged neighbors sued. The sheik and his wife split, the house was gutted by an arson fire, and the sheik skipped to Miami, where he ran up a huge tab at the Diplomat Hotel which he paid only after being thrown in jail. In 1983 a Los Angeles court awarded the sheika $3 billion, the largest divorce settlement in history, but it was later reduced to $81 million, of which the sheik paid only a few million, barely covering her legal fees and forcing her to file for bankruptcy.

❖ LESLIE WEXNER, chairman of the Limited, Inc., purchased a 21,000-square-foot Manhattan townhouse for $13 million in 1989 and spent millions more on renovations. The house, which was the subject of an *Architectural Digest* cover story, has heated sidewalks and a secret, lead-lined bathroom with a telephone and closed-circuit TV monitors concealed in a cabinet. But for some reason Mr. Wexner has chosen not to occupy the residence. Amid much speculation, the interior designer John Stefanidis has offered an explanation: "He now goes to New York very, very seldom, and some people just don't have the time to live in all their houses."

Following a tour of the magnificent thirty-nine-room mansion of publicist and art and celebrity collector Benjamin Sonnenberg, the dramatist Tennessee Williams briefly excused himself to go to the bathroom. Later, according to Ben Sonnenberg, Jr., Williams said, "It looked so shabby when I took it out, I couldn't go."

LANCE DAVIDSON, *The Ultimate Reference Book: The Wit's Thesaurus*

they live in good neighborhoods

Aspen, Colorado

Aspen has become a country club for the very rich. It is Beverly Hills in the mountains. Galena Street looks like Rodeo Drive. The Ute City Banque restaurant, with men and women decked out in mink parkas and Gucci accessories, looks like Ma Maison. You even hear people talk deals. And Aspen is 100 percent international. English is almost a second language.

JEAN VALLEY, *Rocky Mountain Magazine*

Beverly Hills, California

We figured out everybody in Beverly Hills would qualify for food stamps. The president says if you own $1,000 in personal property, you're not eligible. Well, nobody in Beverly Hills owns anything, not even a pot or a pan. Everything is leased.

MORT SAHL

Once I was coming down a street in Beverly Hills and I saw a Cadillac about a block long, and out of the side window was a wonderfully slinky mink, and an arm, and at the end of the arm a hand in a white suede glove wrinkled around the wrist, and in the hand was a bagel with a bite out of it.

DOROTHY PARKER

Brentwood, California

Social note: at the restaurants [in Brentwood], alfresco dining is passé; shade is in—not because of u.v.'s but because one side effect of the new families of antidepressants is photosensitivity. Another altered relationship between body modification and socialization: it is no longer considered improper to appear in public greased with post-cosmetic surgery Polysporin, nose plasters or wrap-around dark glasses.

DOUGLAS COUPLAND

Fairfield County, Connecticut

The town rang with gimcrackery, human as well as material. There were the new owners of old shore properties, people with allergies and two-toned cars, who had built swimming pools on the beaches. They sat around them eating frozen canapés and drinking gin-and-tonics with weekend guests who arrived on Thursday.

PETER DE VRIES, *The Tents of Wickedness*

Grosse Pointe, Michigan

Detroit, in the minds of Grosse Pointe people, exists as a gray area where some men have to go for business, and from which they escape at night.

STEPHEN BIRMINGHAM, *The Golden Dream*

Jupiter Island, Florida

About twenty miles north of Palm Beach there is a smaller, tighter enclave of very rich families, mostly "old family." People who live there usually say they are from Hobe Sound. That is an "in" joke. Hobe Sound is a mishmash of social levels. The really elite area doesn't start until you cross the bridge to Jupiter Island.

After you have been to Palm Beach, Jupiter Island really isn't much to look at. There are about four hundred houses along two roads, with a nice golf course occupying the space between the roads. People mostly have their names on their mailboxes. If they go calling at night it may be in a two-decades-old wooden station wagon. You can see most of the houses and the houses you see are mostly handsome well-tended one-stories, some spread out but very few awesome by Palm Beach standards. About the only thing an outsider can buy on the island is a newspaper or liquor. The main island dock is too small to handle jumbo yachts.

Yet over the decades Jupiter Island has been populated by people who have such names as Mellon, Marshall Field, du Pont, Harriman, Whitney, Ford, Duke, Doubleday, Heinz, Dillon. . . . Average

they live in good neighborhoods

per family net worth certainly would be more than $15 million. . . . You don't have to go through any gate to get onto Jupiter Island, but as I was cruising down Gomez, one of the two roads, I was going slowly to check out the houses. Within moments a police car pulled up behind me. I resumed normal speed and was not bothered. There is a policeman for every sixteen houses. If you stop to get out and walk past some trees to get a better view of the outer shore, you are apt to have your car towed away. Sensors along the roadside, I was told, notify a central police monitor if any car has stopped along the road.

VANCE PACKARD, *The Ultra Rich*

It's no good going to Jupiter Island unless one also owns a house and belongs to the Jupiter Island Club. Both these privileges remain firmly within the suzerainty of Mrs. [Joseph Verner] Reed. The prospective candidate for admission must first pass three probationary winters on the island, allowing Mrs. Reed the opportunity to observe the applicant's deportment. If at any time during those three winters Mrs. Reed finds anything amiss, she sends her butler to the candidate with the gift of a new cashmere sweater. The sweater is for the trip north.

LEWIS H. LAPHAM, *Money and Class in America*

La Jolla

It costs a lot of money to live in La Jolla.

RAYMOND CHANDLER

Main Line (Philadelphia)

On the Main Line, Radnor is considered "very nice." "Very nice is another way of saying filthy rich" says one Main Line resident.

STEPHEN BIRMINGHAM, *The Golden Dream*

Monaco

For eight centuries, Monaco has been, as one wit called it, "a sunny place for shady people." During World War II, Rainier's grandfather, Prince Louis II, saved the family fortune by collaborating with the Nazis who turned Monaco into a furlough base for German troops. Holding companies were set up so that Goering, Himmler and other top Nazi officials could launder money.

JON ANDERSON, *Chicago Tribune*

Nantucket

The rich came to Nantucket in search of a refuge and turned it into the very world they were trying to escape. Such is the curse of the rich. Like Midas, they are doomed to destroy the fragile beauties they love by turning them into tonnages of gold.

RUSSELL BAKER

New Canaan, Connecticut

New Canaan is a town with a common (Wasps love to think they are New England born and bred, even if they aren't). New Canaan is also a town where life is built around "the club" (with long waiting lists; Wasps often must join second-rate and even third-rate clubs). At Friday-night buffets and Saturday-night dances, the Wasps of New Canaan gather together in tribal rituals for which the women are carefully dressed (never flashily—that's for New York) with little white pearls on their swanlike necks. Waspy women don't seem to age: they just weather from the sun, sea, and drink.

JOHN FAIRCHILD, *Chic Savages*

Newport, Rhode Island

The summer playground of America's upper crust during the Gilded Age. Its harbor was the anchorage for fabulous yachts; its stately marble mansions on Bellevue Avenue, also known as "Millionaire's Row," with domestic servants who outnumbered the occupants, were disingenuously called "cottages" by their occupants. Real estate taxes and the high cost of help have forced their owners to open them to the public, and in season busloads of tourists pay $7 each for a glimpse at nineteenth-century American opulence.

Oscar Wilde described Newport as a place "where idleness ranks among the virtues." Henry James saw it as a "little white hand which had suddenly been crammed with gold," and upon visiting it after a long absence he described the effect of its concatenation of magnificent mansions:

What an idea, originally, to have seen this miniature spot of earth, where the sea-nymphs on the curved sands, at the worst, might have chanted back to the shepherds, as a mere breeding ground for white elephants! They look queer and conscious and lumpish—some of them, as with an air of the brandished proboscis, really grotesque— while their averted owners, roused from a witless dream, wonder what in the world is to be done with them. The answer to which, I think, can only be that there is absolutely nothing to be done; nothing but to let them stand there always, vast and blank, for reminder to those concerned of the prohibited degrees of witlessness, and of the peculiarly awkward vengeances of affronted proportion and discretion.

HENRY JAMES, *The American Scene*

New York, NY 10021

The section of Manhattan encompassing Park, Madison, and Fifth avenues, bordered by Sixtieth Street to the south and Eighty-sixth Street to the north, contains perhaps the greatest concentration of luxury apartments in the world, many of which have fabulous views of Central Park and house museum-grade art collections behind unassuming facades.

Buyers of multimillion-dollar co-ops must often pay for them in cash and demonstrate a net worth of at least three times the purchase price, and they frequently spend an amount equal to the purchase price to redecorate.

Palm Beach, Florida

Palm Beach looks like hell on wheels, Rolls-Royce of course, where every face is lifted, and many of the jewels, where in winter they sleep in their sables, where life's a ball, a party, but don't drop dead on the dance floor—not without a photographer, because the only really dead people in Palm Beach are those whose pictures no longer appear in the local papers.

RONALD HASTINGS, *Daily Telegraph* (London)

Santa Barbara, California

Many were the black sheep of their respective families and were encouraged to go to California by relatives who were eager to have them transplanted several thousand miles from home. This accounts, Santa Barbarans say, for the special *laissez-faire* of the place—less grand and pretentious than Newport, less formal and competitive than Palm Beach.

STEPHEN BIRMINGHAM, *California Rich*

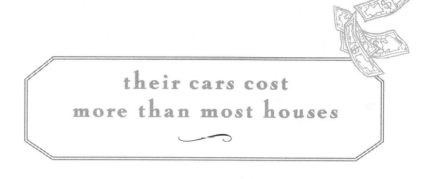

their cars cost more than most houses

In one of the most effective ongoing marketing campaigns of all time, the manufacturers of the Rolls-Royce have created a mystique around their product, which has transcended the status of a mere automobile: The Rolls-Royce is an institution, a universally recognized status symbol, the epitome of automotive luxury. (Never mind that Vickers PLC, the Rolls-Royce parent, unable to finance a new engine development program, had to make a deal with BMW to supply engines.)

Lots of small details contribute to the mystique: The company boasts that the leather for each "motor car" comes from cattle raised inside electronically fenced enclosures rather than behind barbed wire "to prevent abrasions." The canard that every Rolls is delivered with a sealed hood still persists. And white gloves are included in the tool kit, presumably so the owner can keep his hands clean should he ever be so unfortunate as to have to change a tire himself.

The Bentley buyer tries to have it both ways. Since everyone knows a Bentley costs just as much as a Rolls and is identical except for the massive grille and trademark "flying lady" hood ornament, the Bentley owner achieves two contradictory effects: the conspicuous consumption value of a Rolls, and credit for not being "ostentatious."

Palm Beach County, Florida, has the largest number of Rollses per capita in the nation—one for every 13,000 citizens. The Principality of Monaco has the largest number per capita in the world—one for every 65 subjects, though it's safe to assume that the Rollses belong to the international tax refugees in residence there and not to native Monegasques.

Rolls owners run the gamut from rock stars to maharajahs, sheiks to heads of state, gurus (Bhagwan Shree Rajneesh had 93) to monarchs (the sultan of Brunei had 165 at last count).

As of this writing, the entry-level Silver Dawn costs $150,000; a Rolls limousine $350,000; the Bentley Azure $340,000.

There was a time when Ogden Reid's garages were reduced to a practically irreducible four Rolls-Royces. It had been the occasional habit of the publisher of the *Herald Tribune* on emerging from Bleeck's during the evening to enter the car handiest to the saloon's swinging door, a conveyance not always his. On opera nights when Fortieth Street was crowded with parked motors, all of them of superior make, it wasn't always possible for the Reid chauffeur to obtain a position directly in front of Bleeck's and, since all town cars looked very much alike at night, Mr. Reid sometimes popped himself into Robert Goelet's Packard or Mrs. S. Stanwood Menken's Isotta. This occasion for confusion was eventually overcome when Arthur Draper, for many years the publisher's confidential assistant, arranged to have all four Reid Rolls-Royces take up adjacent positions at the curb on Fortieth Street during the dinner lull in traffic, thus eliminating all possibility of contretemps since almost any car he might select on leaving the bar would be his own.

LUCIUS BEEBE, *The Big Spenders*

their cars cost more than most houses

they travel
first-class

When he [Averell Harriman] was only 8, his dad, railroad king E. H. Harriman, took it into his head that he wanted to shoot a Kodiak bear. When a Harriman conceived such a wish, it was not just a matter of heading for the Arctic, hiring a professional hunter, finding a bear and killing it. Harriman *père* set out for Alaska at the head of an expedition, 126 strong, complete with hunters, botanists, artists, stenographers, taxidermists, a chaplain and John Muir, the founder of the Sierra Club.

GODFREY HODGSON, *Los Angeles Times Book Review*

Each guest had a great Indian double tent, bigger than most London drawing-rooms. The one tent was pitched inside the other, with an air-space of about one foot between to keep out the fierce sun. Every tent was carpeted with cotton, and completely furnished with dressing-tables and chests of drawers, as well as writing-table, sofa and arm chairs. . . . The Census of 1891 was taken while we were in camp, so I can give the exact number of retainers whom the Maharajah brought with him. It totalled 473, including mahouts and elephant-tenders, grooms, armourers, taxidermists, tailors, shoemakers, a native doctor and a dispenser, and boatmen, not to mention the Viennese conductor and the thirty-five members of the orchestra.

LORD FREDERIC HAMILTON, on tiger hunting with the maharajah of Cooch Behar

❖ NUBAR GULBENKIAN, the son and heir of the fabulously rich oilman Calouste Gulbenkian, was a classic *bon viveur* who lived the life of an Edwardian dandy (the London papers dubbed him "the Last Magnifico"). Gulbenkian ordered a limousine custom-made from a high-roofed London taxicab to accommodate his top hat. "The car can turn on a sixpence," he bragged, "whatever that is."

❖ DIAMOND JIM BRADY bought for his mistress, the music hall star Lillian Russell, a gold-plated, diamond-and-pearl-encrusted bicycle for jaunts around Central Park. When she went on tour, the bike accompanied her in a custom-made Moroccan leather travel case.

❖ WHEN THE LATE Time Warner boss Steve Ross flew his wife and two other couples to Mexico one Christmas, the trip required two corporate planes: One for people and one for gifts.

Money was not the end for this man at all, money was a very peripheral thing for him. Beating the odds, winning the game, that was his objective. He was a numbers man. He lived by the numbers, he took an elevator by the numbers, he came into town by the numbers.

Everything was done by the numbers. When he left his house in the morning he did not leave at 8:10, he left at 8:07. All of the policemen knew—because of his time schedule—that he would be going down Fifth Avenue say at 8:37. Of course, traffic lights were hand-operated then by policemen on boxes. So, the instant that they saw his car, the lights were green. He never stopped for a red light.

PATRICIA LIVERMORE, of her father-in-law, Jesse Livermore

A private railroad car is not an acquired taste—one takes to it almost immediately.

MRS. AUGUST BELMONT, wife of the New York businessman who financed the IRT subway

◈ E. F. HUTTON once spent $5,000 to have his wife Marjorie Merriwether Post's private railroad car filled with orchids.

John Hay Whitney owned an old Fairchild prop plane painted green and white to resemble his Long Island home, Greentree. Its interior had been done by Sister Parish with mahogany paneling and tweed upholstery. It was old and slow, but elegant and grand. Guests likened it to traveling on the Orient Express. When Bill Paley invited the Whitneys to Nassau aboard his new Gulfstream II, the CBS founder suggested they send their Fairchild down with the luggage. Whitney had a better idea: "Bill, why not send your plane down with the baggage," he said. "It could be unpacked and pressed by the time we get there."

❖ THE ARMS DEALER Adnan Khashoggi had a DC-8 with a sunroof in the master bedroom and a window in the floor of the breakfast cabin (which presumably gave him the illusion of floating on air while having his corn flakes). There were fiber-optic light switches embedded in the carpeting and onboard laser beams for in-flight light shows. On one occasion Khashoggi, a large man, chartered a second jet to transport a supply of bottled water he used for bathing.

❖ DONALD TRUMP'S 727 had 24-karat-gold seat-belt buckles (creditors forced him to sell the jet in 1990).

❖ BUNNY MELLON ROTATES paintings from her collection onboard her Gulfstream II. She is reputed to have once sent the plane from Antigua to Guadeloupe to do grocery shopping.

❖ ON A TRIP TO London with Kleenex heir James H. Kimberly and his wife, a companion was astonished to learn that the Kimberlys' fifteen Louis Vuitton trunks were filled with Kimberly-Clark toilet tissue. "Jim refuses to use any other brand," Mrs. Kimberly explained.

The Duchess never became a Queen but she had done her best to live like a Queen. She and the Duke had once traveled with insouciance through a war-torn Europe taking with them no less than 222 suitcases, and that was not counting all her extra hat and jewelry boxes.

Their entourage was enormous, it resembled an unaffiliated army, it included so many maids carrying lapdogs that belonged to the Duchess. When the Windsors arrived at stations, journalists were sent to meet them in order to get photographs of Wallis Windsor's monumental pile of luggage.

CAROLINE BLACKWOOD, *The Last of the Duchess*

The idea of a form of transport that is at the same time highly visible to the mob and yet insulated from it remains as seductive as ever. And the most satisfying contemporary example of that is the coal-black stretch limousine. (White is vulgar, gray is a compromise banker's color, puce and magenta and antique crackle-finish gold are not for gentlemen. It has to be black.)

There is something almost indecent about using several yards of machinery and the full-time services of another human being simply to move you the short distance between lunch and your next appointment. This, of course, is one of the most rewarding aspects of travel by stretch, but not one you would necessarily want to mention to liberal acquaintances who are concerned about equality, ecology, and our moral obligation to use mass transit.

PETER MAYLE, *Acquired Tastes*

There was always a feeling of warm entitlement that came with riding in a limousine. Griffin was used to it; it was impossible to feel a kinship with ordinary people in dented, rusted cars with uncomfortable seats. If he lost the job, perhaps this would be the privilege hardest to give up. Yes, and he envied the really wealthy, who had private limousines, for whom the privilege was not an illusion.

MICHAEL TOLKIN, *The Player*

I began to dread rides in the family limousine, a long black Chrysler. When [the chauffeur] took me to school in it, I slid down in the front seat, trying to stay out of the view of the group of my classmates who bicycled to school each day along the same route. I timidly tried to talk to Father about this. He listened solemnly—he always heard me out, never interrupted anybody. But when I was finished, he declared, "Well, Adam, I just don't think having a car like that is anything to be ashamed of."

ADAM HOCHSCHILD, *Half the Way Home: A Memoir of Father and Son*

THE TEENAGE DORIS DUKE'S limousine was equipped with a panic button she could push whenever a boy tried to kiss her.

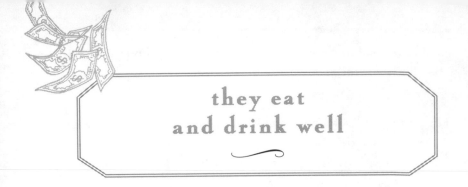

they eat and drink well

The late André Sella, proprietor of the Hotel du Cap d'Antibes, told me this story: "I remember one of dose rich Russians, Count Apraxine. He had many *manies* [idiosyncracies]. One was to have sent to his salon every night a dozen fresh strawberries on a silver dish. Fresh strawberries was hard to find in Chanuary in dose days—I am talking of nineteen two, t'ree, along dere. Dey cost ten gold francs apiece, but de count, he don't care. And we'n de strawberries are browt every night, w'at you t'ink he did? He squeezed dem wit' a fork, and we'n dey are all squeezed, he *smell* dem. 'Ah!' he say, taking deep breat. 'A-*ha!*' and den he go to bed . . . No, he did not eat dem. He chust squeezed dem. I t'ink people who have too much money, dey are alwiss a lettle crazy."

     J. BRYAN III, *Hodgepodge*

Ina selected from her salad a leaf of Bibb lettuce, pinned it to a fork, studied it through her black spectacles. There is at least one respect in which the rich, the really very rich, *are* different from . . . other people. They understand *vegetables*. Other people—well, anyone can manage roast beef, a great steak, lobsters. But have you ever noticed how, in the homes of the very rich, at the Wrightsmans' or Dillons', at Bunny's and Babe's, they always serve only the most beautiful vegetables, and the greatest variety? The greenest petit pois, infinitesimal carrots, corn so baby-kerneled and tender it seems almost unborn, lima beans tinier than mice eyes, and the young asparagus! the limestone lettuce! the raw red mushrooms! zucchini. . . .

TRUMAN CAPOTE, "La Côte Basque"

One day we went down to the cellars with Wilcox and saw the empty bays which had once held a vast store of wine; one transept only was used now; there the bins were well stocked, some of them with vintages fifty years old.

"There's been nothing added since his Lordship went abroad," said Wilcox. "A lot of the old wine wants drinking up. We ought to have laid down the eighteens and twenties. I've had several letters about it from the wine merchants, but her Ladyship says to ask Lord Brideshead, and he says to ask his Lordship, and his Lordship says to ask the lawyers. That's how we get low. There's enough here for ten years at the rate it's going, but how shall we be then?"

EVELYN WAUGH, *Brideshead Revisited*

they eat and drink well

Even for those who dislike Champagne, myself among them, there are two Champagnes one can't refuse: Dom Pérignon and the even superior Cristal, which is bottled in a natural-colored glass that displays its pale blaze, a chilled fire of such prickly dryness that, swallowed, seems not to have been swallowed at all, but instead to have turned to vapors on the tongue and burned there to one damp sweet ash.

TRUMAN CAPOTE, "La Côte Basque"

❖ BEFORE HE BECAME a recluse, Howard Hughes liked to dine at various Hollywood restaurants, including Chasen's, where he invariably ordered steak, mashed potatoes, and peas. He always carried a strange utensil that looked like a small, silver rake, which he used to separate the peas from the mashed potatoes and steak.

they really know
how to party

I played a party in the 80's, believe it or not, where a man gave a bar mitzvah, listen to this, on the QE2. He hired the entire ship. She went out to sail with 650 guests. He had the entire class of his kid. As he pulled into the harbor, to show you the type of fellow he was, Ivan Boesky landed in his helicopter. So that sort of pins this guy, right? He's now broke, by the way.

PETER DUCHIN, *New York Times*

The nouveaux riches accepted the [New York Metropolitan Museum's] invitation [to hold lavish parties there in return for "donations"] and within two short years, they had converted it into a sort of arena for their own status rituals, a circus for the enactment of social ambition. Parties were held there evening after evening after evening. During the fall of 1988 . . . Marvin Traub, the head of Bloomingdale's, threw a party at the museum for Robert Campeau, who had recently acquired the department store in a hostile takeover battle for its parent company. John Gutfreund, the head of Salomon Brothers, and his wife Susan, held a cocktail reception. Henry Kravis, who would negotiate the $25 billion leveraged buyout of RJR-Nabisco that same fall, and his wife, the clothes designer Carolyne Roehm, had a sit-down dinner for 140 people. Social columnist Billy Norwich found himself writing so often about the shindigs and hoo-has at the museum that he took to referring to it as Club Met.

JOHN TAYLOR, *Circus of Ambition*

◈ ALVA VANDERBILT'S COSTUME BALL in 1883 was so highly anticipated that when Mrs. Astor learned that her daughter had not been invited, she paid a personal call on the parvenue Mrs. Vanderbilt to secure her an invitation, and in so doing established the Vanderbilts for ever after in New York society.

◈ THE BRADLEY MARTIN BALL, February 6, 1897, held at the Waldorf-Astoria during a nationwide economic slump, is said to have cost between $250,000 and $400,000. Guests were invited to come dressed as royal courtiers. (Mr. Martin went as Louis XV.) Attended by the cream of New York society, with every sumptuous detail reported by the yellow press, the ball created so violent a public backlash that the Martins fled to England, never to return to the United States.

◈ AT THE WEDDING of Rita Hayworth and Aly Khan in 1949 at *l'Horizon*, his villa on the French Riviera, some five hundred guests consumed fifty pounds of caviar and six hundred bottles of champagne while Yves Montand sang. As a special touch, the swimming pool had been filled with several hundred gallons of perfume.

◆ THERE MAY NEVER have been a more opulent party than the shah of Iran's 1971 wingding celebrating the founding of the Persian Empire by Cyrus the Great 2,500 years earlier. It was attended by 450 guests including scores of royals, heads of state, and international celebrities. The food came from Maxim's of Paris, which flew 150 chefs to Iran to prepare caviar-stuffed quail's eggs and foie gras–stuffed roast peacock, along with a platoon of wine stewards to dispense 25,000 bottles of vintage wines in Baccarat crystal. Housed in sixty-two air-conditioned tents spread over 160 acres, the party is estimated to have cost $100 million.

◆ FOR HIS SEVENTIETH birthday in 1989, with Elizabeth Taylor as his "date," the late magazine publisher Malcolm S. Forbes flew seven hundred friends and business associates to Tangier for a lavish black-tie affair at Forbes's *Palais de Mendoub.* The guests, including William F. Buckley, Jr., Henry Kissinger, Donald Trump, Walter Cronkite, Rupert Murdoch, and Robin Leach, arrived courtesy of Forbes on three jetliners, a DC-8, a 747, and an Air France Concorde.

      The entertainment included a 274-man Moroccan Cavalry honor guard and hundreds of belly dancers and drummers. Two hundred waiters washed the guests' hands before the feast.

Though the cost was estimated at $2 million, a good time was not had by all: Some VIP's had to stand in line for hours for tent assignments, while those guests lodged at the Hotel Solazur said the rooms smelled of fish. Others complained of the lack of ice and the inability to get a cup of coffee. William F. Buckley, Jr., said that he had been more uncomfortable physically than at any time since he left infantry basic training, and Liz Smith likened the experience to "taking an un-air-conditioned bus trip with 700 people to Ardmore, Oklahoma over the dog days."

◈ GAYFRYD STEINBERG'S GALA fiftieth-birthday party for her husband Saul in 1989 was titled "An Evening of Seventeenth Century Old Masters in Celebration of Saul's Fiftieth Year." The event was held in a replica of a seventeenth-century Flemish tavern and featured live models *en tableau vivant* as old-master paintings.

Mr. Steinberg was less than grateful. During the festivities, perhaps anticipating the hundreds of thousands of dollars the party would cost him, he told his wife, "Honey," he said, "if this party were a stock, I'd short it." The Steinbergs were divorced a few years later.

◈ THE NUPTIALS OF the daughter of Saul Steinberg and the son of Laurence Tisch at the Metropolitan Museum of Art in New York featured 12,000 white tulips, 50,000 French roses, a forest of dogwood branches, gold-dipped magnolia leaves, a hand-painted marbleized dance floor and a $17,000 wedding cake, at a total estimated cost of $3 million.

◈ AT A TIME when his own newspapers were railing against the excesses of the mighty rich, Joseph Pulitzer imported the entire New York Symphony Orchestra for a dinner party at his Bar Harbor estate.

◈ THE SULTAN OF BRUNEI flew the Teenage Mutant Ninja Turtles to London for his son's ninth birthday party at a cost of $1 million.

◈ WHEN HIS TWO CHILDREN were small, the television producer Aaron Spelling had snow trucked in for their annual Christmas party.

◈ DURING THE 1980s, New York hostess Carolyne Roehm (then Mrs. Henry Kravis) substituted the traditional common coins with rare silver ones in her Christmas plum pudding.

But There Are Exceptions

Marjorie Merriwether Post was a problem. She wasn't really social, but she was very rich, and her house, Mar-a-Lago, was the biggest in Palm Beach, so she couldn't be ignored. She gave terrible parties, and her Thursday-night square dances were universally dreaded, though attending them was a must. They were carried out with parliamentary precision, with Mrs. Post barking out the orders in her loud midwestern twang. Guests were expected at the doorstep of Mar-a-Lago precisely at 7:30, not a minute earlier or a minute later. Once they had all flocked in, each guest was served no more than two drinks. At 8:00 sharp, dinner was announced, and those whose invitations read "cocktails only" were ordered to leave, while the rest were seated. Mrs. Post's meals were undistinguished. Chicken hash was a favorite entrée. At precisely 9:30 P.M., guests were marched toward the ballroom, but before entering they had to remove their shoes and don satin slippers, thus to protect Mrs. P's highly-waxed ballroom floor. Then, *everybody* had to square dance. No wallflowering or resting between sets was permitted. On the dot of eleven, the music stopped, and guests were told to go home.

STEPHEN BIRMINGHAM, *Vanity Fair*

Playboys

Now virtually extinct, they thrived between the end of World War II and the late 1960s, when their exploits were the stuff of gossip columns. They were dashing young men who had inherited wealth but not responsibility—second or third sons in a tradition which gave the firstborn the family business—so they devoted their lives to the pursuit of pleasure. They displayed the savoir faire and the insouciance of the very rich at a time when bland conformity was the rule. Lucius Beebe limns the quintessential playboy in his description of James Gordon Bennett:

A playboy with $1,000,000 income a year after taxes . . . a libertine whose mere presence could cast doubt on the reputations of women of otherwise unassailable virtue, a voluptuary who remained as brandied and incandescent as a Christmas pudding for years on end, and, in addition to these qualifications for attention, proprietor and sole owner of two of the world's most successful daily newspapers, James Gordon Bennett was not a personality to pass unnoticed. . . .

Along the French Riviera of the nineties and in the gentlemen's clubs of Paris after the turn of the century, he found companionship worthy of his mettle. Durable Russian grand dukes were handy who could take over the conduct of Maxim's for an evening as a *beau geste* and foot the bill in doing it. Younger sons of English lords schooled in the horsemanship of long country ancestry could keep up with his demented coaching. Amiable playboys of a dozen nationalities were on tap to participate in his expensive practical jokes, and the revenues from the *New York Herald* and the prestige of the *Paris Herald* excused everything.

LUCIUS BEEBE, *The Big Spenders*

◈ HUNTINGTON HARTFORD WAS the grandson of George Huntington Hartford, founder of the Great Atlantic & Pacific Tea Company, which grew into the A&P supermarket chain. After being raised in Newport and graduating from Harvard in 1934, he joined the A&P statistics department, but was soon fired for various infractions, including sleeping on the office floor and taking a day off to attend the Harvard-Yale football game.

With an income of $1.5 million a year, he became one of New York's most notorious playboys whose antics—for example, he liked to go out in bedroom slippers instead of shoes and drink milk in nightclubs—often made the gossip columns.

He would squander the $100 million he inherited in 1958 on various pet projects: he started a modeling agency and stood on street corners handing out business cards to prospective clients; he wrote a play and spent $500,000 to have it produced on Broadway, only to have its star, Errol Flynn, back out at the last minute; he spent another $500,000 to establish an artist's colony in Pacific Palisades, California (nobody came); he spent $7 million on an art museum in Manhattan that closed for lack of interest; he founded a magazine called *Show* which cost $8 million before it folded in 1964; he bought Hog Island in the Bahamas for $11 million, renamed it Paradise Island, and spent another $20 million to build a golf resort, but despite massive publicity it never caught on and he had to sell it in 1966 at a huge loss.

He was married and divorced four times, though his last ex-wife remained loyal to him. By the time he reached his seventies, he had been reduced—or rather had reduced himself—to living in a squalid Manhattan townhouse on $400 a week.

❖ HUGH HEFNER, the founder-publisher of *Playboy* magazine, is included on this list only because he popularized the word "playboy": his origins were too middle-class and he worked too hard for his money to deserve the sobriquet himself.

◈ PHILIPPE JUNOT SPECIALIZED in princesses, including Caroline of Monaco (Frank Sinatra sang "My Way" at their wedding), Sophie de Hapsburg, and Beatrice von Auersperg. He retired at the age of forty-seven, when he married a twenty-five-year-old Danish beauty. "For me it is very important to have one woman in my life. To be with someone on a steady basis. It gives balance to a man's life to know there is someone at home he can be quiet with."

◈ ALY KHAN WAS the eldest son of the Aga Khan, the spiritual leader of some 15 million Ismaili Muslims, who showered him with riches, including his weight in precious gems and gold as part of a devotional ceremony known as *tula-vidhi*. His Italian mother, a former ballerina, was the second of the Aga Khan's four wives.

Aly Khan rode to the hounds, drove in Grand Prix races, hunted big game, and piloted his own plane. He set a long-distance record in 1932 when he flew a radioless, single-engine craft from Bombay to Singapore, later describing the dangerous trip as "fabulously fun." In the pre-credit-card era, he kept the safe in his Mediterranean villa crammed with the currencies of a variety of countries so he could fly off at a moment's notice to anywhere he wished. He married Rita Hayworth in 1949, but they were divorced two years later. In 1960 he died in a sports car crash at the age of forty-eight.

◈ WHILE THE TERM "Welsh playboy" may seem oxymoronic, Dai Llewellyn, who inherited a fortune in Wales real estate from his father, was a frequent target of the British press because of his philandering—the tabloids dubbed him "Seducer of the Valleys."

◈ PORFIRIO RUBIROSA WAS the prototypical "big dame hunter," marrying a succession of heiresses, including Flor Trujillo, the daughter of the dictator of Rubirosa's native Dominican Republic; Barbara Hutton—the marriage lasted seventy-three days; and Doris Duke, during which ceremony he smoked a cigarette. One clue to his popularity: in jet-set circles, elongated restaurant pepper mills were known as "Rubirosas." He died a playboy's death in 1965, when he crashed his Ferrari into a tree in the Bois de Boulogne.

◈ GÜNTHER SACHS, a German automobile heir, is most famous for marrying Brigitte Bardot (she called him "Saxy"') in a Las Vegas ceremony which he attended sans socks. They were divorced after three years.

they're picky

◈ LEONA HELMSLEY HAD her sheets ironed daily, and upon finding a wrinkle in the bed linen she would summon a maid to re-iron and remake the bed.

◈ IVANA TRUMP REPORTEDLY so abhors footprints on the carpets in her home that she requires a room to be freshly vacuumed before she will enter it.

◈ MRS. ELECTRA WAGGONER WHARTON of Dallas could not abide clothing that had been tried on by anyone else, so the ever-obliging Neiman Marcus had frocks sent to her directly from its couturiers in Paris, still in their original packages with the customs seals unbroken.

At the Pacific Union Club in San Francisco the kitchen staff scours all the coins brought into the building by members tainted with the commerce of the streets. Only after the coins have been thoroughly polished do the waiters presume to offer them as change on silver trays.

LEWIS H. LAPHAM, *Money and Class in America*

French dress designers, hairdressers, and cooks are admitted to be unbeatable, but they lose their eye, their hand, their skill after a few years in England or America. Why? Because they are no longer under the disciplinary control of *les femmes du monde*—that is to say, of a very few rich, ruthless, and savagely energetic women who know what they want and never spare anybody's feelings in their determination to get it.

NANCY MITFORD

Bunny [Mellon] is a perfectionist and has been known to take on young painters, who work for years on the floors and walls of her houses in New York, Cape Cod, and Antigua. Her floors are painted with shadows, so that on a dreary day the sunlight still seems to be streaming through. Her vegetable garden is laid out on the bias, and her gardening clothes are designed by Givenchy himself.

JOHN FAIRCHILD, *Chic Savages*

After pressing my nose up against the window and watching [the rich] in action from time to time, I'm not at all sure they enjoy themselves as much as we think they do. And why? Because, damn it, something is always *not quite right*.

Expectations tend to increase in direct proportion to the

they're picky

amount of money being spent, and if you're spending a fortune you expect perfection. Alas, life being the badly organized shambles that it so often is, and with so much of it dependent on the behavior of erratic equipment (servants), perfection is rare. After a while, the rich realize this, and they start looking for trouble. I've seen them do it. Details that we would consider trivial assume enormous significance: the breakfast egg is inedible because it is marginally underboiled, the silk shirt is unwearable because of a barely visible wrinkle, the chauffeur is insupportable because he's been eating garlic again, the doorman is either insufficiently attentive or overly familiar—the list of maddening blots on the landscape of life just goes on and on. How can you have a nice day if some fool hasn't warmed your socks or ironed your newspaper properly?

PETER MAYLE, *Acquired Tastes*

For some of the tenants at 100 Central Park South, hardship is not being able to get a table at Le Cirque on thirty minutes' notice. If I've learned one thing about the rich, it's that they have a very low threshold for even the mildest discomfort.

DONALD TRUMP

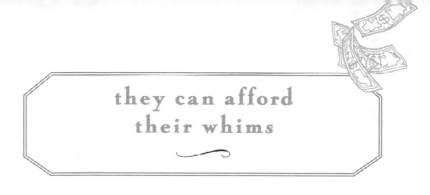

they can afford their whims

Oddest shoot I ever saw was in Russia, in the Perm District, just beyond the Urals. Nineteen twelve. We shot all morning: snipe, white partridges, woodcock, blackcock, wolves, Siberian roebuck, and heaven knows what else. Then caviar and vodka. Then a picnic luncheon, course after course, all served on priceless Sèvres, and washed down with vintage champagne. When the tables had been cleared, the host lined up all the servants and told us, "Now we'll have some *real* shooting!" And damme if they didn't toss that Sèvres into the air for us to pot! "Shoot!" he said. "You'll enjoy it! The china's quite good quality." Imagine! Sèvres clay pigeons!

COLONEL FREDERICK CRIPPS, quoted by J. Bryan III in *Hodgepodge*

◈ VIEWERS ARE TOLD by Morley Safer in a 1973 *60 Minutes* piece that a Saudi Arabian prince and his three bodyguards are bound for Syria on the Orient Express "to shoot swans with a chromium-plated sub-machinegun."

◈ CALOUSTE GULBENKIAN WAS A fabulously successful middleman who became known as "Mr. Five Percent" after he secured himself a one-twentieth share in the Iraq Petroleum Company. In 1930 he spent several million dollars to purchase, and hundreds of thousands to maintain over the succeeding years, a 150-acre garden near Deauville, France, which he visited just once a year.

◈ FRANK J. GOULD, an American millionaire who in the 1930s turned the quiet Mediterranean village of Juan-les-Pins into a fashionable resort, took a ten-piece band with him wherever he went so he could always hear his favorite tunes.

◈ HAROLD FARB, THE "Apartment King of Texas," once paid the Houston Symphony $25,000 to accompany him in a Gershwin concert, and he reportedly spent $100,000 to cut his own record album, *An Evening with Harold Farb.*

◈ WILLIAM WALDORF ASTOR had his office release the false news of his death so he could read his own obituaries.

◈ VINCENT ASTOR HIRED actors to pose as waiters and spill soup on his friends.

❖ RICHARD BRANSON, THE BRITISH entrepreneur whose Virgin Records, Virgin Atlantic Airways, and Virgin Megastores have made him a billionaire, enjoys practical jokes. On April Fools' Day in 1989, after fitting one of his hot-air balloons with running lights and a false façade to disguise it as a UFO, he landed in a field near London, whereupon a midget dressed as ET emerged, to the utter astonishment of the police, army units, and paparazzi who had mobilized to follow it.

❖ DORIS DUKE, WHO GAVE a coming-out party for her two pet camels, both of which had the run of her mansion, once had a ton of seaweed shipped from Newport, Rhode Island, to her house in New Jersey—to put in her bath water.

❖ JENNINGS BRYAN OSBORNE, JR., a multimillionaire owner of a biomedical research company, has become one of the most notorious citizens of Little Rock, Arkansas. His 22,000-square-foot house there has been the center of controversy since he started decorating it in 1986 with millions of Christmas lights. The displays include a flashing, thirty-foot globe, a working calliope, Mickey Mouse driving a Christmas choo-choo, computerized snow, and the words "Merry Christmas" and "Happy New Year" in letters six feet high.

The two-acre, million-dollar walled estate where Osborne lives with his wife, Mitzi, and his daughter, Breezy, has become a popular tourist attraction. When U.S. Supreme Court Justice

Sandra Day O'Connor visited Little Rock in 1994, she asked to see two things: the Arkansas River and the Osborne Christmas display.

When his immediate neighbors began complaining about the noise and commotion, Osborne bought the two adjoining houses to silence them, then decided to use the houses to triple the size of the light show. But other residents of the affluent suburb complained that during the holiday season the thousands of sightseers cruising by the Osborne house had turned their neighborhood into a "Yuletide Disneyland." It was so bad, they claimed, it often took an hour just to get to the neighborhood convenience store.

Osborne responded by doubling the number of lights in the display, and the neighbors sued for public and private nuisance. The case went all the way to the Arkansas Supreme Court, which ruled in favor of the plaintiffs and required Osborne to mute the lights and sound effects to the point where they don't attract crowds or otherwise disturb the neighbors. Osborne appealed unsuccessfully to the United States Supreme Court, then donated the lights to Walt Disney World. Asked why he did it, he replied, "Just making memories for Breezy."

◈ JAMES MARION WEST, JR., a Texas oilman, was nicknamed "Silver Dollar Jim" because he liked to scatter silver dollars on the ground and watch people scramble for them. He also loved to ride around in Houston police cars armed to the teeth wearing a sheriff's uniform. His $100 million estate included a horde of 290,000 silver dollars and 41 Cadillacs.

Pleasure is worth what you can afford to pay for it.

WILLIAM RANDOLPH HEARST

Howard Hughes was able to afford the luxury of madness, like a man who not only thinks he is Napoleon, but hires an army to prove it.

TED MORGAN

Ross Perot bought his boyhood home in Texarkana and preserved it. The bricks of his home had been painted white, so he asked that they be sandblasted. The sandblasting did not work, so he ordered the house torn apart and the bricks turned around so that their unpainted sides faced outward.

RICHARD LOUV

At the Hotchkiss School I knew a boy who chose to imagine himself a gunfighter on the old Oklahoma frontier. It was a charade that he carried out with immense solemnity, and never once do I remember being so gauche as to make a joke. From a tailor in New York he ordered several suits in the style of the 1870's; at Abercrombie and Fitch he bought an authentic Colt revolver that had once belonged to a cavalry officer stationed at Fort Leavenworth during the Indian Wars. He also acquired a hat, a string tie and boots. During school vacation he fought gun duels with the western heroes prominent in the early days of television. The butler would roll the television set into the drawing room and the boy, whose parents were invariably attending a charity or masquerade ball, would dress himself up in the nostalgia of the Old West. Standing at what he thought was a sporting distance from the screen he would wait, his right hand held slightly above his holster, for the moment when the good guy faced the bad guy in the deserted, dusty street. The boy fired at whichever of the two figures drew his gun against the camera. Afterwards he poured himself a drink in the library while the butler cleared away the broken glass.

LEWIS H. LAPHAM, *Money and Class in America*

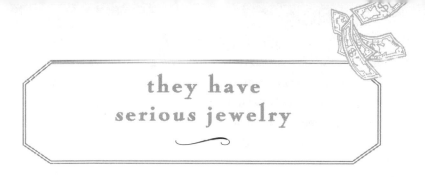

they have serious jewelry

◈ MRS. HORACE DODGE had a six-foot-long necklace made of 389 matched, marble-size pearls that had once belonged to Catherine the Great.

◈ MRS. ELEANOR SEARLE WHITNEY'S string of matched pearls the size of pigeon's eggs was originally owned by the Empress Eugénie.

◈

Mrs. Ronald Greville (1867–1942), heiress to a Scottish brewing fortune and a popular London hostess, did not take kindly to guests whose jewelry was more "important" than her own. After dinner one evening a rich American discovered that a large diamond had fallen from her necklace. Everyone got on their hands and knees to look for the stone, except Mrs. Greville, who haughtily offered a magnifying glass and announced, "Perhaps this will help."

◈ MRS. ROBERT GUGGENHEIM'S sapphire, at 424 karats, was so heavy that it could only be worn clipped to specially reinforced evening dresses.

❖ TRUMAN CAPOTE'S "Black and White Ball" at New York's Plaza Hotel in 1966 was the social event of the decade. One of the few complaints came from Gloria Guinness, who said that she regretted having worn two heavy necklaces—one diamond and one ruby—the combined weight of which had exhausted her, requiring her to stay in bed all the next day to regain her strength.

❖ MRS. EVA STOTESBURY TOOK pains to avoid wearing the same jewelry twice: she maintained an elaborate log detailing the precise combinations of rings, necklaces, bracelets, and tiaras she wore on specific occasions and dates.

❖ THE DEPARTMENT STORE TYCOON Gordon Selfridge gave each of the two Dolly Sisters a four-carat blue diamond set in the shell of a live tortoise.

❖ IN 1987 THE LATE duchess of Windsor's jewels were sold at auction by Sotheby's for just over $50 million.

❖

Mrs. Louisine Havemeyer (1855–1929) built a fabulous art collection which she donated to the Metropolitan Museum of Art. When asked by a wealthy friend why she wasted her money on "little dabs of paint," Mrs. Havemeyer looked at the woman's pearl necklace and replied, "I'd rather have something made by a man than something made by an oyster."

they really know how to shop

In reckless extravagance he outdid the prodigals of all times in ingenuity, inventing a new sort of baths and unnatural varieties of food and feasts. He would bathe in hot or cold perfumed oils, drink pearls of great price dissolved in vinegar, and set before his guests loaves and meats of gold, declaring that a man ought either to be frugal or Caesar. He even scattered large sums of money among the Commons from the top of the Julian Basilica for several days in succession. He also built Liburnian galleys with ten banks of oars, with sterns set with gems, particolored sails, huge spacious baths, colonnades, and banquet-halls, and even a great variety of vines and fruit trees. In these he would feast even in the daytime amongst singers and dancers as he coasted along the shores of Campania. He built villas and country houses with utter disregard of expense, caring for nothing so much as to do what men said was impossible. So he built moles out into the deep and stormy sea, tunneled rocks of hardest flint, built up plains to the height of mountains and razed mountains to the level of the plain, all with incredible dispatch, since the penalty for delay was death. To make a long story short, vast sums of money, including the 2,700,000,000 sesterces which Tiberius Caesar had amassed, were squandered by him in less than the revolution of a year.

SUETONIUS, "Gaius Caligula"

❖ MARIE ANTOINETTE, LOUIS XVI'S queen, was known as "Madame Deficit" for her profligacy at a time when there were bread riots in the streets of Paris. She kept a dressmaker on retainer for the equivalent of a million dollars a year, and

Every winter she would order twelve gala dresses, twelve formal dresses, and twelve simple dresses, plus linen and muslin dresses for summer, as well as a wide variety of accessories and ornaments. The gala gowns were usually embroidered with either gold or pearls at an estimated cost of 1,000 francs per gown. . . . [She] was especially infatuated with jewels. Many she bought on credit, and once, even though she had already exceeded her annual allowance by double, she purchased a pair of bracelets for 200,000 francs, then went to her husband, the king, to ask for a loan to help pay for them (he grudgingly helped her). Another time she swapped some of her diamonds to buy a pair of chandelier diamond earrings for 400,000 francs. When her own mother warned her about her buying habits, she told her not to worry, that it was just a "bagatelle."

M. HIRSH GOLDBERG, *The Complete Book of Greed*

◈ IN NOVEMBER 1994 the homebuilding tycoon Eli Broad bought Roy Lichtenstein's *I ... I'm Sorry* at a Sotheby's auction for $2.5 million, paid for it with his American Express card, and earned 2.5 million frequent-flyer miles in the bargain.

◈ ON ONE VISIT to a London jeweler during the Arab oil embargo, the sultan of Dubai bought a hundred pairs of solid gold cuff links and five diamond-encrusted Piaget watches at a total cost of £800,000.

◈ IN ONE DAY OF shopping Harry and Leona Helmsley bought furniture for their Connecticut mansion, including a card table for $210,000, a side table and chairs for $140,000 and a highboy for $150,000 ... and charged it all to their hotels. According to a former maid, Mrs. Helmsley bought stockings by the gross and lipstick by the case.

◈ IN A SINGLE afternoon of shopping in New York when she was still the first lady of the Philippines, Imelda Marcos reportedly bought $234,000 worth of antique jewelry, a $100,000 diamond necklace, and a $43,000 silver tea service. During her racketeering trial, the U.S. government alleged that she spent $6,671,919 on jewelry between 1980 and 1986.

    According to a friend, "if she liked something, whether it was chocolates, silk blouses, the finest bags or shoes, she would buy ten dozen, and when she was not sure whether she liked something, only five dozen." When the Marcoses were voted out of office in 1986, and the doors of Malacañang Palace were thrown open by the new president, her closets held thousands of pairs of shoes, 500 bras, and 2,000 dresses, prompting Congressman Stephen Solarz of New York to comment that "compared to her, Marie Antoinette was a bag lady." (In 1992, five years after her exile from the Philippines, Mrs. Marcos was observed in New York buying six pairs of crocodile pumps at $1,000 a pair.)

❖ JACQUELINE ONASSIS WAS known as a "speed shopper" who could spend $100,000 in ten minutes. She reportedly once bought two hundred pairs of shoes in one brief sortie. Truman Capote recalled accompanying her on what he called a "shop-till-you-drop spree": "She would walk into a store, order two dozen silk blouses in different shades, give them an address and walk out." She reportedly spent over $600,000 on Persian rugs and jewelry during a week-long visit to Teheran, after which an exasperated Aristotle Onassis (whose accountants nicknamed her "Super-tanker" for her huge capacity for luxury cargo) dropped her monthly allowance from $30,000 to $20,000.

❖ *In a famous anecdote, Henry Luce questions his wife, Clare Boothe Luce, about a $7,000 lingerie bill and she replies, "Well, Harry, are we wealthy or aren't we?"* ❖

The Robb Report

Founded in 1971 as a newsletter for people who buy and sell classic cars, the *Robb Report* has become what its publisher calls "a full service lifestyle magazine for affluent and upscale people," devoting its pages to "the tastes and interests of the most affluent readers in the world, addressing the privileged lifestyle of the self-made man." Though its popularity may have peaked in the eighties, the *Robb Report* claims a monthly circulation of 120,000 for its thick, glossy magazine that sells on "selected" newsstands for $6 a copy.

The editorial content of the *Robb Report* is minimal. The few articles are designed to complement the ads. Thus recent issues include a report from the Paris Auto Show featuring full-color photos of a new Mercedes-Benz roadster, a puff piece (as it were) on the increasing popularity of "cigar dinners," and a column entitled "Investibles" touting the rewards of antique corkscrew collecting. But the ads are what give the *Robb Report* its character.

The publisher's claim that *Robb Report* readers have "more disposable income than the readers of any other magazine in the United States," is reflected by the full-color ads for "connoisseur motorcars," corporate jets, and "luxury estates." In the market for a customized Lincoln Town Car stretch limo? It's yours for $350,000. Your automotive tastes a little sportier? There are dozens of new and used Ferraris and Lamborghinis to choose from. Ashtrays full in your Learjet? The Aero Toy Store has everything from Hawkers to Gulfstreams. Looking for that perfect weekend hideaway? Premium Properties offers a 2,000-acre ranch on California's Monterey Peninsula complete with its own airport for $15 million. And if you really want to get away from it all, 2,100 acres of lush New Zealand countryside with a small lake, an airfield, and "a lovely meandering stream" can be yours for only $4,950,000.

But there are even more exotic goods and services advertised in the *Robb Report*: Want to fly a MIG-29 at Mach 2 over Moscow? Supersonic Holidays will help you "join the most elite flying club in the world" (from $3,100). Need to "Cover Your Assets" with hidden surveillance? Qüark Spy Centre offers over sixty-five custom products, including video cameras disguised as lamps, clock radios, and baseball caps. Need a guard dog that's gentle with the kids? The two-page ad for Dawn Roller's Best Pets' Neopolitan mastiffs ("bred to bond with your most valuable assets—your family and your home") is quintessential *Robb Report*. It features color photographs of satisfied celebrity customers (including Joe Piscopo and "Don Diamont, Television Actor of 'The Young and the Restless'") and the headlines YOUR FAMILY'S BEST FRIEND, THE INTRUDER'S WORST NIGHTMARE, WE CATER TO AN ELITE SET OF CLIENTELE WHO APPRECIATE PERFECTION, and WHEN ONLY THE BEST WILL DO, YOU CAN'T GET BETTER THAN THE BEST!!!!" [*sic*]. A color photo of the fetching Ms. Roller bears the credit: "Photo by Rudolph Henninger/Hair by Daniel at Youngbloods."

Then there are the classifieds, for everything from antigravity waterfalls to a lawyer who provides "significant Nevada tax-free strategies" to a service which promises to show you how to obtain a second passport and teach you

> *how to become a P.T. (PERPETUAL TRAVELER).*
>
> *Live cheaply without working. Bargain paradise guide. Avoid lawsuits. Make enough to retire in 3 years. Legally avoid taxes. How to buy new cars for half price. Free brochure.*

There are classifieds for rare coins, vintage wristwatches, handcrafted hood ornaments, miniature horses, men's hairpieces, a "dependency management program for the affluent," a mail-order specialty shop for "serious *Playboy* collectors," and "TP for the VIP":

> *Custom imprint the name of your boat, airplane or business on full-size rolls of toilet tissue. We will also print your personal-*

ized message for birthdays, anniversaries, sporting events or meetings—anything you can imagine. Send a photo, news clipping, logo, or special quote. You will receive 8 beautiful rolls of custom-imprinted toilet tissue for $49.95 plus S/H. Inquire about our political TP.

But perhaps the most telling *Robb Report* ad bears the simple headline CREDIT PROBLEMS?

A sampling of the gifts listed over the years in the Robb Report's *annual "Ultimate Gift Guide":*

- A sterling silver tennis ball can for $1,750.
- The "world's most expensive bow tie" in 24-karat gold with 22 karats of inlaid diamonds for $140,000.
- A man's BMW logo ring for $2,750.
- A small cashmere throw rug with the Mercedes-Benz logo imprinted on it for $2,000.
- The world's only complete Winchester Commemorative collection (seventy-five guns) for $299,000.
- A custom-designed pair of Tony Lama boots with 384 diamonds, rubies, and other precious stones sewn into English calfskin for $32,000.

- Your own personal bowling center (installed) for $75,000.
- A mink coat for a Cabbage Patch Kid for $400.
- An 18-karat-gold Space Traveler's Watch which displays mean time, star time, the age and phase of the moon and is designed to "entertain space voyagers as they tour the galaxy," for $350,000.
- A working 24-karat-gold-plated gumball machine set with 158 diamonds, rubies, emeralds, and amethysts for $100,000.
- A crocodile-skin chewing-gum holder for $250.
- The Flarecraft 370, a thirty-foot boat that goes airborne and skims the waves at 72 mph for $60,000.
- A one-on-one with Michael Jordan or a shift on the ice with Wayne Gretsky for "$100,000 to $2.5 million depending on athlete."

they're greedy

People seem to enjoy things more when they know a lot of other people have been left out on the pleasure.

RUSSELL BAKER

A prominent banker who was financier André Meyer's contemporary still marvels at his "almost erotic attachment to money. Just to have it, to feel it, to be in possession of it gave him an enormous kick. Money was the symbol of success, and it was the symbol that attracted him, and not the practical use of it." Money wasn't there for spending but for keeping score, to assure him that he was winning.

CARY REICH, *Financier, The Biography of André Meyer*

The love of money as a possession—as distinguished from the love of money as a means to the enjoyments and realities of life—will be recognized for what it is, a somewhat disgusting morbidity, one of those semi-criminal, semi-pathological propensities which one hands over with a shudder to the specialists in mental diseases.

JOHN MAYNARD KEYNES, "Economic Possibilities for Our Grandchildren"

Cornelius Vanderbilt attended a séance expecting to receive financial advice from his deceased partner, Jim Fisk, but the spirit of Vanderbilt's departed wife showed up instead. "Business before pleasure," he told her. "Let me talk to Jim."

He heaps up his money in his heart, where the heartbeats can count it.

ELIAS CANETTI

Money is my first, last and only love.

ARMAND HAMMER

I must keep aiming higher and higher, even though I know how silly it is.

ARISTOTLE ONASSIS

they're greedy

Anyone who thinks greed is a bad thing, I want to tell you it's not a bad thing. And I think that in our system, everybody should be a little bit greedy. . . . You shouldn't feel guilty.

IVAN BOESKY, at the height of his success

It's a sickness I have in the face of which I'm helpless. . . . I am deeply ashamed and I don't understand my behavior.

IVAN BOESKY, to Judge Morris E. Lasker, just before he was sentenced to a three-year prison term for securities fraud

they have domestic servants

One nice thing about being rich: You ring a bell and things happen.

GARY COOPER, summoning a servant in *Mr. Deeds Goes to Town* (screenplay by Robert Riskin)

If the rich could hire other people to die for them, the poor could make a wonderful living.

YIDDISH PROVERB

Averell Harriman consulted the distinguished CBS commentator Charles Colling-wood on a matter of public relations over breakfast one morning, after which Colling-wood offered to drive Harriman downtown. When Collingwood got behind the wheel, Harriman sat in the back and began to read his newspaper.

THE CHAUFFEUR TO Mike Bendum, the "King of the Wildcatters," amassed a $17-million fortune by keeping his ears open for oil stock tips while driving his employer.

◈ THE POTTER PALMER mansion on Lake Shore Drive in Chicago had no outside doorknobs. Entry could be achieved only when an ever-present servant opened the door from the inside.

◈ AT THE TURN of the century, Mr. and Mrs. Henry Fowler McCormick, first-generation heirs to the McCormick reaper fortune, dined lavishly in the Empire Room of their mansion on Chicago's Lake Shore Drive. Menus for family meals were always in French, and four servants were routinely employed to serve luncheon for two.

I leave the cooking to those who have more time.

CAROLINE HUNT

◈ MRS. EVA STOTESBURY kept a personal couturier on staff at her suburban Philadelphia estate to sketch her wearing various costumes so she could see how she might look in a given ensemble without having to endure the drudgery of actually trying the clothes on.

◈ SIR JAMES GOLDSMITH'S estate in Careyes, Mexico, has its own police force and a squad of servants whose only job is to kill scorpions.

Mrs. [Gayfryd] Steinberg and I frequently differed on management technique. I preferred one based on trust; she preferred one based on humiliation. Gayfryd would not allow any of the staff members to lock the doors to their rooms. Eventually, I found out why: When they were out, she would enter the tiny maids' rooms and search through their closets. If the rooms were untidy she would chastise the girls for their slovenliness. Not one to trust the competency level of her staff, Gayfryd would hide various items behind curtains and under furniture and then check later in the day to see if the maids had cleaned properly and removed the hidden items. I had been supervising domestics for years but had never encountered such dehumanizing tactics.

DESMOND ATHOLL, *At Your Service: Memoirs of a Major Domo*

Asked why she was carried everywhere by a burly attendant, Barbara Hutton replied, "Why should I walk when I can hire someone to do it for me?"

---

they have domestic servants

they have yachts

Rich people are nuts for boats. The first thing that a yo-yo like Simon LeBon or Ted Turner does when he gets rich is buy a boat. And, if he's high-hat kind of rich—that is, if he made his money screwing thousands of people in arbitrage instead of screwing hundreds selling used cars—he buys a sailboat.

P. J. O'ROURKE

In New London, the early morning of 21 June 1935 was overcast and foggy, but when the wind came around to the southeast, the sun appeared, the fog lifted, and the fleet was revealed. The [presidential yacht] *Sequoia* was surrounded by hundreds of boats: slim, powerful tenders, whose brass and brightwork gleamed in the sun; catboats and schooners, the working vessels of Arcadia fitted out for the summertime ordeals of the rich. Among them all, the big yachts rode at anchor like chaperones at a debutante ball. There were at least sixty vessels in the 150–250-foot range, from Charles E. F. McCann's 248-

foot *Charlena* to Ogden Mills's *Avalon,* Ernest Dane's *Vanda,* Mrs. William L. Harkness's *Cythera,* Cornelius Vanderbilt's *Winchester,* Alfred B. Sloan's *Rene,* Edward S. Harkness's *Stevena,* and so on down to a 150-foot yacht from Texas owned by a Dr. John R. Brinkley and called, to the derisive laughter of the avatars of good taste around her, the *Dr. Brinkley II.* The *Nourmahal* was missed, as was her owner. (Vincent was commodore of the New York Yacht Club that year, but his half-brother, John Jacob VI, whom everyone called Jackasster, was the only Astor in the news that day. He'd been seen at Bailey's Beach in Newport, having just retrieved *the* Mrs. Astor's diamond ring from an enraged former fiancé.) Still, even without the *Nourmahal,* a *Times* reporter happily noted that the yachts at New London composed the largest flotilla of private vessels ever assembled. Old Money, he might have added (but didn't), was doing very well in the Depression.

NELSON W. ALDRICH, JR., *Old Money*

Any man who has to ask about the annual upkeep of a yacht can't afford one.

J. P. MORGAN, JR. (Attributed)

Because it's the most expensive, yachting beats all other recreations as a theater for upper [class] status exhibition. But certain inviolable principles apply. Sail is still far superior to power, partly because you can't do it simply by turning an ignition key and steering—you have to be sort of to the manner born. (Probably the most vulgar vessel you can own is a Chris-Craft, the yachting equivalent of the Mercedes.) The yacht must be quite long, at least thirty-five feet, and in getting a new one you must constantly trade up, never down. According to one yacht broker, boat status proceeds by five-foot increments. The customers, he says, will "jump up five feet at a time until they get up to sixty or seventy feet." And the yacht should aim at the uncomfortable racing style rather than the dumpy, folksy, family style, which might suggest living on it all the time, thus hinting at privation. For this reason houseboats are at the class bottom, like trailers, failing on at least three counts: if movable, they're moved by power, not sail; they're comfortable boats with lots of room; and one lives on them. In smaller racing yachts of the higher classes, archaism and internationalism figure. Because they're old and unlocal, the Star and the six-meter have lots of status.

In the matter of the material yacht hulls are made of you can see the two essential principles which confer class on objects, organicism and archaism, operating together as they do so often. Boats made of wood are classier than boats made of the cheaper and more practical fiberglass: the stuff they are made of was once alive, and when boats are made of it they have the status of virtual antiques, like Oriental rugs. And when repairs or replacements are necessary, they're more expensive.

PAUL FUSSELL, *Class*

◈ CORNELIUS "COMMODORE" VANDERBILT'S *North Star* cost $500,000 in 1853. At 2,500 tons, it was more ocean liner than yacht, as the typical sailing yacht of the day measured 50 or 100 tons. The staterooms were paneled with genuine rosewood and appointed with Neopolitan granite and yellow marble from the Pyrenees, and the vessel was heated by a then revolutionary steam system. The *North Star*'s complement included a ship's doctor and chaplain.

◈ JAY GOULD'S *Atalanta* had a superb library, an upright piano in the music room, and a Viennese pastry chef. Guests were ferried from the landing in cutters manned by uniformed oarsmen and were "piped" aboard navy style.

◈ NED GREEN BOUGHT a 225-foot, 2,000-ton Great Lakes steamer, had it cut in two and an additional 40 feet of length added so that it would be the largest private yacht in the world. The *United States* had a crew of seventy, ten powered lifeboats, and nine master suites. The main cabin, decorated in a Jacobean motif, had a fieldstone fireplace.

◈ MRS. RICHARD CADWALADER of Philadelphia commissioned a 408-foot private vessel, *Savarona*, which would be twice the length of the largest oceanliner of the day. When it was completed and Mrs. Cadwalader discovered that the yacht lacked elevators, she refused delivery and ordered them installed at an additional cost of $1 million dollars.

◈ JAMES GORDON BENNETT'S *Namouna* had a live cow tethered on the foredeck in the unlikely event that the newspaper magnate would require milk during a voyage. Bennett named his other yacht *Lysistrata*, he explained, "after a Greek lady who was reported to have been very beautiful and very fast." Its amenities included a Turkish bath complete with steam rooms, cold showers, and a masseur on duty around-the-clock.

Guests aboard the *Lysistrata* were subject to the Commodore's tyrannical whims in a degree which makes one wonder if the free grouse, plovers' eggs, and champagne were worth the price in inconvenience and indignity. No planned itinerary was ever available or even thinkable and the vessel stayed at sea for as long or brief a time as suited the owner's vagrant fancy. Sometimes he put off on protracted voyages with guests aboard who had only been invited for a cocktail or afternoon tea. Once at Amsterdam an entire musical-comedy company was hired to provide entertainment for what they imagined to be a brief interlude while the vessel was in port and only discovered when they had removed their costumes and make-up that they were out of sight of land. After the hysteria had abated, the mummers mingled on terms of egalitarian camaraderie with the bogus dukes and down-at-heels duchesses who constituted the ship's regular sailing list and were returned to port the next morning. Not only did the Commodore pay them handsomely for their fright but reimbursed the management of the theater for the money it had been forced to refund at the box office.

LUCIUS BEEBE, *The Big Spenders*

❖ THE 1,600-TON *Valhalla*, owned by the Count and Countess de Castellane (née Anna Gould) had a crew of ninety.

❖ IN 1954, ARISTOTLE ONASSIS spent $4 million to remodel a Canadian navy frigate and named it the *Christina* for his only daughter. It had lapis lazuli fireplaces in the staterooms, nine "luxury suites" with Venetian mirrors and solid-gold fixtures, a Gauguin, a Pissarro, and two El Grecos hanging on the bulkheads, and in the lounge . . . barstools made from the scrotums of sperm whales.

❖ STAVROS NIARCHOS'S 380-foot *Atlantis* had a swimming pool, a forty-seat movie theater, and a helicopter pad.

❖ MALCOLM FORBES'S 151-foot *Highlander* carried a helicopter and two speed boats.

❖ DONALD TRUMP BOUGHT Adnan Khashoggi's 282-foot vessel for $30 million in 1982 and renamed it the *Trump Princess*. The world's largest private yacht, it was powered by two 3,000-horsepower turbo-diesel engines, and had leather-covered bulkheads, onyx bathtubs, a waterfall, and a discothèque. Trump used it to entertain business associates and high rollers at Trump Castle in

they have yachts

Atlantic City, but not before the Absecon Inlet was dredged to accommodate it. A few years later, his fortunes in ebb, Trump not only had to cancel an order for a new, $110-million yacht, he was also forced to sell the *Trump Princess* at a loss.

◈ THE LATE ROBERT MAXWELL insisted that guests remove their shoes before boarding his 180-foot *Lady Ghislaine*, from which, in 1991, a few days after denying he was an Israeli spy, the bankrupt billion-aire either fell or was pushed or jumped overboard and drowned.

◈ FORMER U.S. TREASURY SECRETARY William Simon's $5-million, 124-foot ketch *Freedom* is equipped with a seventeen-foot, two-man "wet sub." Simon covers the annual upkeep by chartering it three months a year for $45,000 a week.

◈

William Travers, a prominent nineteenth-century lawyer and raconteur, was watching a yacht race at Newport when he realized that all the boats belonged to stockbrokers. "And where are the customers' yachts?" he asked no one in particular.

◈

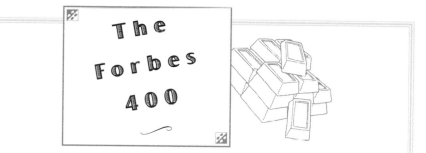

The Forbes 400

The late magazine publisher Malcolm Forbes invented the *Forbes* 400 in the early 1980s and named it to invoke the cachet of the social 400. It has been called the "Miss America Pageant of Wealth," by casual observers, and it has been criticized and reviled by those whose names appear on it and who consider it an invasion of their privacy. (Though other publications estimated his own fortune at anywhere from $200 million to $1 billion, Forbes stubbornly refused to allow himself to be included in the *Forbes* 400 on the rationale that since he didn't know how much he was worth, he would let others estimate it because "people would assume any figure I put down was accurate.")

It's true that net-worth estimates are inherently inaccurate; it is difficult if not impossible to track down foreign assets, or those held through partnerships or corporations. And net worth is often a subjective figure according to how debt is treated: the Texas billionaire

Lamar Hunt once told a *Forbes* editor, "Your list is confused with a list of who owes most."

Many try to get on the list, some try to get off, and *Forbes* receives scores of calls every year from people complaining they are either too high or too low. *Forbes* reporters have been lied to, and there have been attempts to bribe them. Regardless of its reputation, and whether it is accurate or not, the annual *Forbes* 400 issue is always among the most popular of the year.

◈ WHEN THE LATE Wal-Mart founder Sam Walton was first listed (with a net worth of $619 million in 1982), he sent a message to Malcolm Forbes: "I could kick your butt for ever running that list!" After he was ranked the richest man in America four years in a row, Walton complained that his net worth was overstated because *Forbes* included his children's assets. Walton neglected to mention that they had gotten those assets from him.

◈ DONALD TRUMP LOBBIED furiously for position—his high-water mark was $1.7 billion in 1989—to the point, according to Harry Seneker, the *Forbes* editor in charge of the *Forbes* 400, of overstating the value of his assets by hundreds of millions of dollars. Thus when Trump claimed the value of his undeveloped westside Manhattan waterfront property at $650 million, he gave *Forbes* the name of an attorney who *Forbes* thought represented William Zeckendorf, another Manhattan developer, for confirmation. Although a Trump spokesperson denied that there had been any intention to mislead *Forbes*, it turned out that the lawyer worked for Trump, not Zeckendorf. "The richer they make themselves look, the easier it is to make deals with bankers and the easier it is to sign tenants," Seneker explained.

In any case, Trump was off the list a year later, his net worth having plummeted to below zero, according to *Forbes*, after he missed interest payments to the bondholders of Trump Castle in Atlantic City. *Forbes* estimated his debt at $3 billion. Under the terms of a subsequent bailout his creditors took virtual control of Trump's operations and put him on a strict personal allowance.

◈ JENO PAULUCCI, THE FOUNDER of the Chun King Corporation, informed the magazine of some real estate he owned that it had failed to include in its estimate of his net worth, and as a result his position was raised considerably. "I didn't work this hard all my life to be at the pauper's end of the list," he said.

◈ LILA ACHESON WALLACE, the widow of the founder of Reader's Digest, challenged *Forbes*'s valuation of her magazine at $500 million, claiming through her attorney that it was worth only $200 million. When he heard that, Malcolm Forbes told a reporter to "call him back and offer $250 million from me."

◈ THE JOURNALIST Michael Kinsley has observed that only one out of seven on the *Forbes* 400 has earned their fortune in "socially productive" ways.

The wealth of the 400 individuals cited by *Forbes* equals the savings that all Americans have in commercial banks. And that wealth of the 400 is considerably greater than the annual federal budget deficit which has created so much difficulty for the nation. Or take a personal example. The richest man in Arkansas, Sam Walton of Wal-Mart stores, had a net worth in 1987 that was several billion dollars more than his state government's annual budget. He dropped a billion or so in net worth on Black Monday of October 1987 but he shrugged it off as a technical paper loss.

VANCE PACKARD, *The Ultra Rich*

It's a terrible invasion of privacy. It's also very dangerous because it creates the feeling of "haves" and "have-nots." The average person who reads it just sees piles of gold and doesn't realize it's all invested in working capital.

CAROLINE HUNT SCHOELLKOPF, on the *Forbes* 400

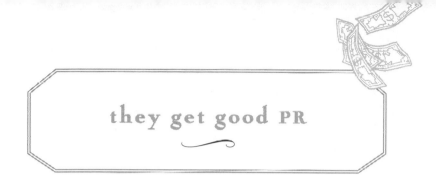

they get good PR

JOHN JACOB ASTOR commissioned Washington Irving to write an account of his exploits in the fur wars of the Pacific Northwest. Titled *Astoria*, it was little more than a book-length apologia for one of the most cunning and ruthless robber barons of the era.

After monopolizing the fur trade Astor began accumulating Manhattan real estate. In 1801 he paid $25,000 for Eden Farm, a tract which encompassed what is now Times Square. Upon his death in 1848 he owned a large percentage of Manhattan, including most of the Lower East Side. His two cardinal rules of real estate investing were (1) own the land, but let someone else take the risk of developing it, and (2) buy wholesale, (i.e., by the acre), sell retail (by the lot).

Not only did this strategy enable the Astors to accumulate even greater wealth, it also gave them a convenient excuse whenever they were confronted with the appalling conditions in the tenements of the Lower East Side. With the wave of immigration in the late nineteenth and early twentieth centuries, these overcrowded, unsafe, and unsanitary buildings spawned great misery, but the Astors could console themselves with the knowledge that they didn't own the *buildings*, just the land. Though they were not slumlords, they were slumlords' landlords. Their carefully maintained image helped make the Astors the leading family in the nation.

❖ JOHN D. ROCKEFELLER hired the public relations wizard Ivy Lee to rehabilitate his image. Rockefeller's name had become synonymous with ruthlessness after his successful campaign to strangle all competition in the oil-refining business, and he had been a favorite subject of political cartoonists, who depicted him as a monster. Lee used staged newsreels to cast Rockefeller as a sympathetic figure, and in a PR masterstroke, created the enduring image of the kindly old gentleman who gave out dimes to little children.

When Adnan Khashoggi, the Arab middleman once called the richest man in the world, held a birthday party for himself at his estate in the hills back of Marbella, Spain, it was an interesting display of splendor. A five-foot-four man weighing about 200 pounds, he brought in a good assortment of European and Hollywood royalty. The theme was Renaissance and guests entered an archway made of crossed swords held up by fifty costumed pages. When the guests finally got

The Rich Are Different

to dining they found an easel at each setting displaying Khashoggi's face beaming from the cover of *Leaders* magazine, which purportedly only goes to heads of state and chiefs of major world corporations. And after dessert an actor dressed as Henry VIII read a proclamation hailing Khashoggi as "the world's greatest." With a flourish, the fifty pages released 2,500 balloons, each with the words "world's greatest" on it.

VANCE PACKARD, *The Ultra Rich*

they get away with murder

Capital cases being the judicial equivalent of neurosurgery, a defendant in a murder trial who can afford the best lawyers—and the attendant experts and investigators—is in little danger of ending up on death row.

Convicted of attempted murder at the first of his two trials, [Claus] Von Bülow within a week of the jury's decision found himself much in vogue on the summer social circuit. His European sang-froid recommended him to those hostesses who liked to serve raspberry sorbet in rooms slightly darkened by an atmosphere of intimate sadism. By September Von Bülow's presence at lunch was as necessary to the afternoon's success as its subsequent description in the gossip columns. Only when he was ultimately acquitted did his luster fade.

LEWIS H. LAPHAM, *Money and Class in America*

◈ IN 1906, Harry K. Thaw calmly shot his wife's former lover, the celebrated architect Stanford White, three times in the head in front of scores of witnesses in a Manhattan restaurant. After a spectacular trial in which the defense put the victim on trial, Thaw was adjudged insane and sent to a mental institution. The wealthy assassin was released after nine years.

◈ ANN EDEN WOODWARD was an ex-showgirl who one night in 1955 blew her wealthy husband's brains out with a shotgun because, she claimed, she thought he was a prowler. She was cleared of murder charges primarily because her mother-in-law, Elsie Woodward, stood by her publicly, though she never believed her story. The case created such a sensation among the international jet set that the Duchess of Windsor remarked, "Nothing like a murder in the country to cure what ails you."

Ann Woodward was thereafter called "Annie-Get-Your-Gun" behind her back. A murderess in Truman Capote's short story, "La Côte Basque," was clearly modeled on her. The day after the story was published in *Esquire*, ostracized by the monied set to which she had worked so hard to belong and exposed to all the world as a killer, she was found dead of a sleeping-pill overdose. Dominick Dunne's 1985 novel, *The Two Mrs. Grenvilles*, which was eventually made into a TV miniseries, is a thinly disguised account of the case.

◈ T. CULLEN DAVIS, a Texas oilman, was tried and acquitted of the murder of his estranged wife's lover and her young daughter in 1976. Despite eyewitness testimony identifying Davis as the killer, the legendary defense attorney Richard "Racehorse" Haynes was able to get Davis an acquittal by attacking the victim for her drug abuse and infidelity. Davis, who has the dubious distinction of being the richest American ever tried for murder, and who used to say that "money can buy anything," certainly got the best justice money could buy. He declared bankruptcy in 1987 and is now a lay minister in Fort Worth.

they're bashable

Other minorities are sacrosanct, but the rich are fair game. Take Leona Helmsley. It's hard to resist taking potshots at a woman who proclaimed herself a "queen" in a series of national advertisements for her husband's hotel chain. She was dubbed "the Queen of Mean" by the tabloids for her treatment of employees, many of whom, according to a government investigator, were only too happy to cooperate in the tax-evasion case against her: "We hardly even had to subpoena people," he said. "People were waiting in line to testify against this woman." (The case had originated with a tip from an unpaid Helmsley contractor.) But Mrs. Helmsley seemed to enjoy the enmity of her staff, somehow regarding it as proof that she was doing her job. She once revealed that her bodyguards had advised her to stay out of hotel kitchens "because there are knives and whew, they hated me."

I confess gladly to being a basher of the rich. A good bashing keeps the rich from becoming insufferable. Not only that, giving them a sturdy bashing makes you feel tip-top if you don't happen to be rich yourself.

RUSSELL BAKER

It is easier for a camel to pass through the eye of a needle than for a rich man to enter the Kingdom of God.

Matthew 19:24

The rich are like ravening wolves, who, having once tasted human flesh, henceforth desire and devour only men.

JEAN-JACQUES ROUSSEAU

Behind every great fortune there is a crime.

BALZAC

The wretchedness of being rich is that you live with rich people.

LOGAN PEARSALL SMITH

The rich are dull and they drink too much.

ERNEST HEMINGWAY

The rich are the scum of the earth in every country.

G. K. CHESTERTON

We may see the small value God has for riches, by the people he gives them to.

ALEXANDER POPE

The Rich Are Different

As a general rule, nobody has money who ought to have it.

BENJAMIN DISRAELI

The only thing I like about rich people is their money.

LADY ASTOR

The rich are not very nice. That's why they're rich.

EDWARD ABBEY

The rich, like well-brought-up children, are meant to be seen, not heard.

LEWIS H. LAPHAM

The world is full of rich shits.

TRUMAN CAPOTE

they're bashable

they're snobs

◈ THE FOUR HUNDRED: The self-appointed social arbiter Ward McAllister (nicknamed "Make-a-Lister" by the newspapers), compiled a roster of the cream of New York society which was published in the *New York Times* on February 1, 1892. McAllister claimed that there were only four hundred people in New York worthy of being called "society" because "if you go outside four hundred, you strike people who are either not at ease in a ballroom or else make other people not at ease." In truth, he had settled on the number arbitrarily: it happened to be the capacity of Mrs. William Backhouse Astor's ballroom. McAllister's snobbism bore the zeal of the arriviste: a man whose patrician credentials consisted entirely of disdaining the American custom of shaking hands, the Four Hundred was *his* entrée to society.

By the 1880's Mrs. Astor had long since dropped her husband's middle name, Backhouse, as not genteel. Now, in the most preposterous act of her career, she decided to drop the first name, William, as superfluous. Henceforth, she instructed her friends and the U.S. Post Office, she would be addressed simply as "Mrs. Astor." Her sister-in-law, Mrs. John Jacob Astor III, was simply amused by Caroline's pretensions, but her humorless nephew, William Waldorf, was so incensed that he tried to seize the name "Mrs. Astor" for his own young wife and, failing in the attempt, removed to England. Caroline, having thus achieved the social annihilation of her own relatives, remained *the* Mrs. Astor to the end of her days.

JOSEPH THORNDIKE, JR., *The Very Rich*

And this is good old Boston,
The home of the bean and the cod,
Where the Lowells talk to the Cabots
And the Cabots talk only to God.

JOHN COLLINS BOSSIDY

❖ IN BOSTON BRAHMIN society, where the Cabots talk only to God, it evidently does not matter that the founding father, John Cabot, who came to Boston from the Isle of Jersey in 1700, made his fortune in slaves and opium.

❖ _____

Asked why he wanted to join the board of Massachusetts Electric, Joseph P. Kennedy replied, "Do you know a better way to meet people like the Saltonstalls?"
_____ ❖

they're snobs

Gridley and I did not become personal friends until my election to the Greenvale Country Club in 1934. I should admit here that election to this club was the social triumph of my life. I never could see why Pussy and the children found it stuffy.

LOUIS AUCHINCLOSS, *"The Fabbri Tape"*

Joseph Alsop, the journalist and collector, once tried to define the social class that Franklin Roosevelt (and he himself) belonged to. After rejecting all the usual epithets—"upper-class," "aristocratic," and the like—he hit upon the class of the "Who was she?" It is true. On their social rounds, Old Money people are always asking one another, of some new wife of a friend, "Who was she?" Old money society is in many ways a man's society, but for breeding purposes it can be extremely concerned with the female line.

NELSON W. ALDRICH, JR., *Old Money*

Just because we walk on their carpets doesn't mean we must dine at their tables.

CAROLINE SCHERMERHORN ASTOR, of the Sloanes, a somewhat less-prominent family that made its fortune selling rugs and furniture

The match between Gerry and Natica was a sensible one. He played his cello while she wrote and painted and they were enormously devoted to each other. To escape *Woodlands*, they moved to the heavily WASP North Shore of Long Island. When they joined the Creek

Club, which banned Jews, Natica became the member of record. Natica didn't regard this as tokenism or as submitting to prejudice, but as pioneering, an assimilationist idea very congenial to Gerald, who would never resolve his conflicted feelings toward Judaism. When his daughter, Geraldine, became one of the few Friedaflix grandchildren to marry a Jew, Gerry was disappointed.

RON CHERNOW, *The Warburgs*

Bertrand Russell, asked his opinion of the incoming British prime minister Anthony Eden, replied, "Not a gentleman. Dresses too well."

The Good Quality Snob, or wearer of muted tweeds, cut almost exactly the same from year to year, often with a hat of the same material, [is] native to the Boston North Shore, the Chicago North Shore, the North Shore of Long Island, to Westchester County, the Philadelphia Main Line and the Peninsula area of San Francisco.

RUSSELL LYNES, *Snobs*

At a fashionable dinner party Grace Vanderbilt was slighted in favor of Nancy Astor, who graciously tried to console her: "It's only because the Astors were skinning skunks long before the Vanderbilts were running ferries," she explained.

Until the year 1883, New York's upper-case musical circles had been contracted in a stoutly defended enclave represented by the production of grand opera at the old Academy of Music in Irving Place. Its boxes, entailed from generation to generation, were the Maginot Line of defense against the onslaughts of new money, and behind its red plush ramparts massed Livingstons, Barclays, Barlows, Beekmans, Schermerhorns, Schuylers, and Duers ranged themselves in hollow square under the joint command of Pierre Lorillard, August Belmont, and Robert L. Cutting. The premises of the Academy of Music permitted only eighteen really advantageous boxes and its structure precluded enlargement, an arrangement which perfectly suited its archaic patronage of breeding instead of money, and conservatism instead of ostentation. Even when William H. Vanderbilt offered $30,000 for occupancy of one of the momentarily available boxes, the hollow square was impervious to assault.

Inevitably the stratagem evolved by Jay Gould in the founding of the American Yacht Club suggested itself. Gould himself was involved to the great social advantage of his family in a group of insurgents which included such perfumed names as William Rockefeller, Darius Ogden Mills, George F. Baker, Collis P. Huntington, and whole shoals of Astors, Roosevelts, and Goelets who were enchanted to join an insurrection that promised once and for all to stamp out a snobbishness of senility in favor of a brave new snobbishness of solvency. Instead of the Academy of Music's parsimonious allowance of eighteen boxes, the new Metropolitan Opera was to have twice that number. The real estate on which it rose at Broadway from Thirty-ninth to Fortieth streets cost $600,000 and the auditorium itself $430,000, and when its boxes, ownership of which cost a tidy $60,000 each, were occupied on opening night, the occupants represented an aggregate wealth estimated by the newspapers of the land at $540,000,000. The circle of boxes was inevitably known as the "Diamond Horseshoe."

LUCIUS BEEBE, *The Big Spenders*

they're snobs

A GENERATION LATER Otto Kahn began giving large sums to the Metropolitan Opera even though as a Jew he could not be assigned a box in the Diamond Horseshoe. Only after many years as the opera's guiding benefactor was he finally permitted to buy one.

Mrs. Isabella Stewart Gardner, whose ancestry went back to a Scottish king who reigned three centuries before the birth of Christ, became impatient with a Boston dowager who was monopolizing the conversation with the exploits of her forbears during the American Revolution. The woman droned on and on, and Mrs. Gardner finally reached the breaking point: "Well," she sniffed, "I suppose they were less careful about immigration in those days."

Snobs talk as if they had begotten their own ancestors.
HERBERT AGAR

Edith Rockefeller, the youngest daughter of John D. Rockefeller and the daughter-in-law of Cyrus McCormick, liked to sign her letters "Edith de la Rockefeller."

It became not to my taste. I would look out my window and see people washing their dishes from the side of the boat.
ROSEMARIE KANZLER, on why she sold her villa in Cap Ferrat

Lord Poole, chairman of the merchant bank Lazard Frères during the 1970s, was asked how he avoided making bad loans. "Quite simple," he replied, "I only lend money to people who've been to Eton."

Interviewed by the BBC after her stepgranddaughter had become princess of Wales in 1981, the romance novelist Barbara Cartland was asked by a reporter whether she thought class barriers were breaking down in England. "Why yes," she replied, "otherwise I shouldn't be sitting here talking to you."

I don't want to be a millionaire, I just want to live like one.
—Old saying

The following advertisement appeared in the December 10, 1994, edition of the *International Herald Tribune*:

> *The once isolated country of Albania is now free and democratic. For men of action, this provides an exciting opportunity to get rich. In the process, you enjoy the pleasures of Europe's last and least-known paradise.*
>
> *In his new report,* How to Become Rich in Albania, *Dr. Gerhard Kurtz reveals the opportunities he's discovered in Albania during recent on-the-spot research into this inexpensive and unspoiled country:*
>
> • *Albania is the poorest country in Europe, but you can live there like a king—even if you're now drawing welfare. Incomes in Albania average $35 a month, so your Western pennies immediately turn into gold nuggets. Suddenly, you can afford everything.*
>
> • *Albania is one of the few countries left where you can lead a feudal lifestyle surrounded by undemanding domestic helpers.*

• *After a half century of being the most repressive country in the world, Albania is sparing no effort to become the world's freest country. Practically everything is allowed.*

• *Albanians are friendly and helpful (Mother Teresa is Albanian!), and they just love foreigners.*

• *Since Albania is too poor to have diplomatic representatives in all countries, any foreigner willing to pay for the upkeep of a consulate or embassy has a chance of being appointed consul or even ambassador.*

• *The Ministry of Education and Culture can offer you a restored noble title, which can be officially documented in your passport for no more than the cost of a mountain bike.*

Find out more about the opportunities in Albania as soon as you can— before other people get there.

they marry for titles

There is no stronger craving in the world than that of the rich for titles, except that of the titled for riches.

HESKETH PEARSON, *The Marrying Americans*

◈ CONSUELO VANDERBILT was forced by her socially ambitious family to marry the duke of Marlborough, whose own family needed cash. It was a lavish affair, marred only by the bride's reticence: she kept everyone waiting a full half hour until she could dry her tears. When she finally appeared, the guests were surprised to discover that she was half a head taller than the groom. The unhappy union ended in divorce after eleven years.

◈ ALICE THAW, HEIRESS to a Pittsburgh railroad fortune, married the earl of Yarmouth. When the couple embarked for their honeymoon in England, they were hotly pursued by a sheriff trying to seize the earl's luggage in lieu of bad debts.

◆ JAY GOULD'S DAUGHTER Anna acquired two titled husbands: she married Count Boniface de Castellane, a Parisian *boulevardier* who systematically squandered much of her fortune, and then divorced him and married the Marquis de Périgord.

◆ GRACE KELLY, THE daughter of a wealthy Philadelphia builder and herself a movie star, married Prince Rainier III of Monaco on April 18, 1956, and became Her Most Serene Highness Princess Grace of Monaco. The lavish wedding was both an international media event and a comedy of errors. The bride's father publicly dismissed his new in-laws as "degenerates," while her mother, a former gym teacher, complained that her jewelry had been stolen. Perhaps not coincidentally, the groom's mother, Princess Charlotte, showed up with René Gigier, the infamous French jewel thief (she thought the air and sun would do him good after his years in prison). The bride and groom later called their wedding a "ghastly experience."

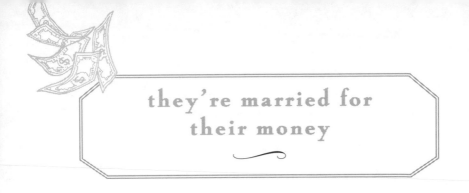

Jacqueline Bouvier Kennedy and
Aristotle Onassis

Though she came from a "good" family, Jacqueline Bouvier was virtually penniless when she married John Fitzgerald Kennedy in 1953. Fifteen years later, when the widowed Mrs. Kennedy shocked the world by marrying the troll-like Greek shipping magnate Aristotle Onassis, a London tabloid bore the headline JACKIE MARRIES BLANK CHECK. Her former brother-in-law, Senator Edward Kennedy, had reportedly negotiated a prenuptial agreement that paid Jackie $3 million up front (i.e., before the wedding) plus a million each for her two children.

After a year or two of marriage their relationship deteriorated; he was reportedly disgusted with her uncontrollable spending, she with his infidelity. It was said that they went from separate beds in the same bedroom to separate beds on separate continents.

Onassis was reportedly contemplating divorce when he died of bronchial pneumonia in 1975. Though his will left Jackie $200,000 a year for life and their prenuptial agreement technically prevented her from claiming the widow's share of the estimated $1 billion estate under Greek law, the threat of legal action led Onassis's daughter Christina to agree to pay her stepmother a settlement of $26 million in cash. (According to Ms. Onassis, Jackie showed up at the funeral with Ted Kennedy, and in the car back from the cemetery he announced that he was sorry to intrude on her grief, but negotiations had to begin immediately). Christina referred to Jackie as "my father's unfortunate obsession" and "the black widow." When the engagement was announced, Christina's brother, Alexander, had remarked, "It's the perfect match: my father loves names, and Jackie loves money." Jackie outlived all three Onassises, and when she died in 1994, her estate was worth $200 million.

Anna Nicole Smith and J. Howard Marshall II

In July 1994, the voluptuous twenty-six-year-old Guess? jeans model and *Playboy* Playmate Anna Nicole Smith married eighty-nine-year-old Texas oilman J. Howard Marshall II, the head of Koch Industries, which is part of a family fortune worth an estimated $500 million. The couple had met at a topless club in Houston.

A few weeks after the wedding, Marshall gave power of attorney to his son, who promptly canceled his stepmother's credit cards

they're married for their money

and stopped payment on a $1 million check his father had written to her. Upon his death a year later, open hostilities between the widow and the family began. They fought over the dead man's ashes (compromise: half to the widow and half to the fifty-four-year-old son) after Smith abandoned her demand that the body be entombed in a pink-marble mausoleum. But there were two funerals, one a quiet service presided over by Mr. Marshall's son and the other featuring Ms. Smith in a low-cut, white side-slit dress singing "(You Are the) Wind Beneath My Wings."

Money alone can't bring you happiness, but money alone has not brought me unhappiness. I won't say my previous husbands thought only of my money, but it had a certain fascination for them.

BARBARA HUTTON

Nobody works as hard for his money as the man who marries for it.

KIN HUBBARD

After the death of his first wife, Los Angeles financier and philanthropist Mark Taper married an actress twenty-eight years his junior. After only eight months Taper sued for divorce on the ground that she had married him "for the sole purpose of obtaining monetary gain."

It is the only bad thing you have ever done. I cannot forgive you.
>   ARISTOTLE ONASSIS to his daughter Christina, upon learn-
>   ing that she had married Joe Bolker, a divorced Los Angeles
>   real estate broker twenty-seven years her senior

Listen, when a billion dollars leans on you, you can feel it.
>   JOE BOLKER, upon his divorce from Christina Onassis after
>   nine months of marriage

they're married for their money

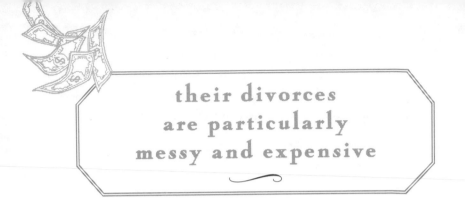

Johnny Carson

His three divorces ran the gamut: In 1959 his first wife, Jody, got $13,500 a year, a '57 Plymouth, and custody of the children. The agreement was amended in 1970 to give her an additional $360,000. In 1972 second wife Joanne got $400,000 in cash and art, $2,000 a week in alimony, and custody of the Yorkie. In 1985, after years of bitter wrangling, third wife Joanna was granted $35,000 a month in alimony for five years, the house in Bel Air, two apartments in New York, a Rolls-Royce, a Mercedes-Benz, stocks, bonds, and 75 gold Krugerrands. Though the Carson divorces were sensational at the time, they're almost quaint by today's standards.

Peter (Herbert Jr.) and Roxanne Pulitzer

The 1982 divorce in Palm Beach featured a bitter custody fight between the former high school cheerleader and the publishing heir over their twin boys, Mack and Zack, amid charges of lesbian sex, occultism, and drug abuse. Roxanne received no money in the divorce, but published several books, including the best-selling *Prize Pulitzer*, and enjoyed a brief career as a quasi-celebrity.

Ivan and Seema Boesky

The once high-flying arbitrageur served twenty-two months in federal prison and paid $100 million in fines and restitution after being convicted of securities fraud in the biggest insider-trading scheme ever uncovered. After she divorced him in 1993 on the grounds of "cruel and inhuman treatment," he sought $20,000 a week in support and half of her $100 million fortune on the grounds that he had made her "rich beyond her wildest imaginings." She claimed she had inherited all her money from her father, who had once owned the Beverly Hills Hotel. After months of public bickering, she agreed to give him $20 million in cash, their house in California, and $180,000 a year for the rest of his life.

Donald and Ivana Trump

After their prenuptial agreement was abrogated by the court (IVANA BETTER DEAL screamed the *New York Daily News*), the parting Trumps agreed to a $14-million settlement which gave her $10 million in cash, a $4-million housing allowance, $100,000 a year in child support for each of their three children, their forty-five-room house in

Connecticut, and the right to occupy their Florida mansion, Mar-a-Lago, one month a year.

In 1995, Donald and Ivana appeared together in a Pizza Hut commercial (for a reported fee of $500,000 each, which they said went to charity). Ivana: "May I have the last slice?" Donald: "Actually, you're only entitled to half."

Sid and Anne Bass

When the Texas billionaire and his wife split up, she reportedly turned down a settlement offer of $500 million. In 1988, after lengthy negotiations, she is believed to have accepted a "package" of cash, art, jewelry, and real estate worth a total of some $300 million.

Edward R. and Elisabeth Broida

In addition to monthly expenses of $5,000 for clothing, $2,200 for hair care, facials, massages, and hair waxing, and $500 for flowers and "home plant care" for herself, the wife of the California architect-developer claimed $8,326 a month in expenses for the couple's six-year-old daughter, including:

Weekday nanny	$2,150
Weekend nanny	860
School uniforms	83
Non-school clothing	1,000
Birthday gifts	400

Beauty parlor	175
Piano lessons	200
Ballet lessons	100
Golf lessons	120
Tennis lessons	120
Equestrian lessons	200
Karate lessons	250

Steven Spielberg and Amy Irving

The director reportedly paid Ms. Irving $92 million in an amicable divorce.

She doesn't have a line in her face—that's what happens when you get ninety million dollars. You look at the check and all the lines disappear.

ARTHUR MILLER

Norman and Francois Lear

The television producer settled a reported $112 million on his former wife, $25 million of which she used to start an eponymous magazine dedicated to independent older women, which folded in 1994 owing thousands to staffers, freelancers, and other creditors.

The Prince and Princess of Wales

Princess Diana received $22.5 million in cash plus a castle in her divorce from Prince Charles, a modest settlement, according to New York divorce lawyer Raoul Lionel Felder: "Princess Di gets a castle and staff and so forth, but the cash is not very much considering her bills, which include $250,000 a year for clothing."

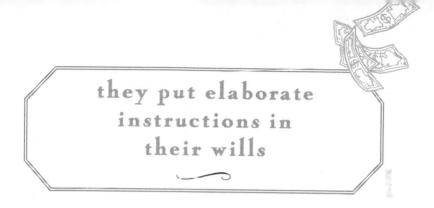

they put elaborate instructions in their wills

It is my desire to be buried in the family burial place prepared by my father in Cedar Hill Cemetery, at Hartford, Connecticut, and I hereby direct that my body be there interred on the west of the monument and opposite the place where my father's remains are interred.

I wish that in all arrangements for my funeral the same general course be followed that was adopted in the case of my father, except that the service shall be held at St. George's Church in the city of New York, with the Bishops of New York, Connecticut, and Massachusetts, and the Rector of St. George's officiating.

J. P. MORGAN

Morgan accordingly left $500,000 to St. George's and $100,000 to the Episcopal Diocese of New York. He also made specific bequests equal to a year's salary to every employee of J. P. Morgan & Company. But the bulk of his $100 million estate went to his son, John, who took over the family business.

◈ ISABELLA STEWART GARDNER'S will requires that her fabulous art collection—she bought Vermeer's painting *The Concert* for $6,000—be displayed in perpetuity in a replica of a fifteenth-century Venetian palazzo. If anything is altered in any way or even moved, the bequest is rescinded and the museum reverts to the Gardner estate.

◈ JOSEPH PULITZER, A Hungarian immigrant who built a newspaper empire on yellow journalism, waxed hypocritical in his will:

> *I particularly enjoin my sons and my descendants the duty of preserving, perfecting and perpetuating* The World *newspaper in the same spirit in which I have striven to create and conduct it, as a public institution from motives higher than mere gain.*

◈ HENRY FORD II affected the common touch:

> *There should be music and the warmth of fellowship and, in this connection, a black jazz band playing "When the Saints Go Marching In" for a recessional, for I do not wish to be remembered only in a solemn fashion.*

◈ NELSON ROCKEFELLER APPARENTLY satisfied a moral obligation:

> *I release and discharge . . . Megan R. Marshack . . . from any indebtedness, including interest thereon, which she may owe to me at the time of my death, and I direct my Executors to cancel any promissory notes or other evidence of her indebtedness to me.*

The amount of "indebtedness" was reportedly $45,000, which Ms. Marshack had used to purchase a co-op apartment. On the night in January 1979 when Rockefeller died of a heart attack, Ms. Marshack was with him in a Manhattan townhouse not far from that apartment. They were said to be working together on a book about his art collection.

◈ WILLIAM S. PALEY, the founder of CBS, took pains to treat his six children equally. He bequeathed each of them $20 million, and when one, his stepdaughter Amanda Burden, borrowed $150,000 to buy a house, he reduced her share accordingly.

◈ JOHN WENDEL, FOR many years a porter to John Jacob Astor, heeded his employer's advice to put his savings in land so diligently that his portfolio of Manhattan real estate was worth $100 million by the time it had devolved to his last descendants, two reclusive sisters named Ella and Rebecca who lived with a series of dogs named Tobey in a brownstone at Thirty-ninth Street and Fifth Avenue. When on one occasion the sisters could not obtain veterinary treatment for an ailing Tobey, they rushed him to Flower Memorial, where a sympathetic M.D. saved the dog's life. The grateful Wendels left $16 million to the hospital.

◈ SANDRA WEST, A WEALTHY Beverly Hills widow, directed that she be buried "in my lace nightgown and my Ferrari, with the seat slanted comfortably."

◈ MALCOLM FORBES MADE specific gifts of $1,000 each to the proprietors of the following New York City restaurants "as a token of gratitude for the joy their skills and genius added to the lives of those who've been lucky and sensible enough to dine at their restaurants": Benihana, Bice, Chanterelle, The Four Seasons, La Grenouille, Le Cirque, Lutèce, Mortimer's, and Nippon. His will also directed that he be cremated and that his ashes be deposited on his private island in Fiji under a stone with the epitaph WHILE ALIVE, HE LIVED.

The Rich Are Different from You and Me

I asked correspondents to complete the second half of the mythic exchange between F. Scott Fitzgerald and Ernest Hemingway— Fitzgerald: "You know, Ernest, the rich are different from you and me." Hemingway: "Yes, I know. They have more money."

No shit, Sherlock.

CHRISTOPHER BUCKLEY

They certainly are, but it'll take more than that to explain Martha Stewart.

DANNY SHANAHAN

The old rich or the new rich? The old rich compete in apathy instead of accomplishment. The new rich are like a sumo wrestler: Having attained the dimensions of a horse, he seeks those of an elephant. He can't stop, even though he's worse off the longer he continues. Money is a form of power, in which men are insatiable. So the very rich accept estrangement from humanity. Of the Rothschilds it was said that they had no friends, only clients.

JOHN TRAIN

They are bored stiff because they don't know where their next thrill is coming from. If Ed McMahon threw the whole Clearinghouse at them, it wouldn't cause a ripple of excitement. Everything is relative. Poor darlings!

PHYLLIS DILLER

They have the burden of spending too much time with the rich.

MORT ZUCKERMAN

Even when they've gone bankrupt, they live better than anyone else.

BRUCE WILLIAMSON

Yes, they are. They smell better, eat better food, live longer, get better medical care, look better, dress better, get better-looking girls, or boys (if that is their preference), wear nicer underwear, and even get a better tombstone. Otherwise, they are exactly the same.

RAOUL LIONEL FELDER

Their cars never break down and their clothes are always clean. Their drivers or butlers simply deal with any problems.

ROBIN LEACH

They never get cold, wet, or hungry.

BILL BLASS

They never wash their own hair.

MARGO KAUFMAN

I certainly agree. I am definitely different now that the money's run out. All I have left is an old school tie and an attitude—the former holding up my trousers, and the latter holding up my career.

IAN WHITCOMB

Yes, they don't have to write any goddamn books.

FLORENCE KING

Yes, but I hope not for long.

MARK ALAN STAMATY

No they aren't, they just want you to think so.

MICHAEL LEWIS

Yes, I know. They don't bother to look how much it costs on the menu.

LIZ SMITH

I know, they're the ones who have gone to the restroom when the check arrives.

EDWARD GOREY

The rich probably are different from you and me, if for no other reason than they spend their lives being treated differently by you and me. Especially in America, where public goods are scarce and private wealth vast, a rich person is a walking piñata. He strolls through life stuffed with surpluses while the rest of us bash away at him with little sticks.

MICHAEL LEWIS

Yes, I know. They had the sense to watch *Wall Street Week* every Friday.

LOUIS RUKEYSER

Yes, I know. They don't wake up at 4 A.M. worrying what will happen to them in their old age.

LIZ SMITH

Yes, I know. They have more lawyers than we do.

ALAN RICHMAN

I know. Rich people don't marry people like Zelda.

JOE QUEENAN

Yes, the rich are different from us. We say money talks. They make money sing.

ROBERT MERRILL

No they aren't. They just think they are because they go to psychiatrists.

MARTIN PERETZ

Yes, the rich are different. They're downright weird. Some observations I've made over the years:

    1. When rich people live in high-rise buildings, the elevator often opens up right into their place!

    2. The rich don't hesitate to have Beluga caviar Fed-Exed to Chappaquiddick Island, something I would never think of in a million years, even if I had the money. (Note: I am not making this up. It actually happened while I was vacationing with rich friends on this prepped-out Fantasy Island. Come to think of it, maybe it was a classic nouveau riche thing to do—the woman who ordered the caviar became frantic that we weren't enjoying it enough and made us all eat it on toast in lieu of lox for breakfast.)

    3. The rich never apologize for the shabbiness of their surroundings.

4. The very rich sometimes have weird bathroom fixtures. When I was a kid, my family was invited to Mary Roebling's mansion (of Roebling Steel) in Trenton, New Jersey, because my sister's dancing troupe had entertained at one of her charity functions. Mary's bathroom had a gilded toilet that was like a stuffed throne with a tufted back. I couldn't use it because I felt like I was peeing in a *chair!*

5. The rich seem to have weird sex lives that center on elaborate nanny fantasies, but I'm just guessing.

CATHY CRIMMINS

Yes, Scott, they are not pussy-whipped by Zelda and never have to prove themselves in the boxing ring, in bed, or on safari.

TAKI THEODORACOPULOS

They really hate poverty.

CHRISTOPHER HITCHENS

Yeah, I know. They labor under the delusion that their shit don't stink.

HARLAN ELLISON

They can afford to run for office.

CHIP ROWE

They think home banking is when a banker comes to your home.

GUY KAWASAKI

They don't take as long to cook.

IAN SHOALES

The rich learn by experience the truth of the old adage, "Money can't buy happiness." The rest of us are expected to take it on faith.

BERTON AVERRE

They have their garage sales at Sotheby's.

MARGO KAUFMAN

How rich?

JOAN SHEPPARD

Glossary

bag-lady syndrome

According to inherited-wealth expert John L. Levy, the panic suffered by rich inheritors when they contemplate losing their money—e.g., "If I were poor, I couldn't survive."

café society

Wealthy New York socialites of the 1930s who frequented such posh night clubs as El Morocco, the Stork Club, and "21."

equestrian class

Rich Americans.

None of the phrases commonly used to describe the holders of American wealth strike me as being sufficiently precise. The United States never has managed to put together an "establishment" in the British sense of the word; "plutocracy" is too vague, and "upper class" implies a veneer of manners that doesn't exist. Borrowed from the Roman usage, equestrian class comprises all those who can afford to ride rather than walk and who can buy any or all of the baubles that constitute the proofs of social status. As with the ancient Romans, the rank is for sale.

LEWIS H. LAPHAM, *Money and Class in America*

family office

An organization which provides various business and financial services for members of wealthy families.

Gilded Age

The period in the United States between 1890 and the start of World War I. It was a time of unbridled optimism and ostentation, of lavish parties at Newport "cottages," the era of the robber barons, trusts, monopolies, and perhaps the last period of unabashed plutolatry in American history.

good catch

A potential mate desirable for his or her money.

There are three key requirements, in addition to money, that go to make up a Good Catch of either sex: The Catch must be (1) ambulatory, (2) straight—unless part of the bargain is a well-paying conspiracy to keep a gay millionaire in the closet and (3) "normal" enough that he or she would not actually be committed to an asylum were the rug of money suddenly to be yanked from under his or her feet.

DIANA McCLELLAN, *Washingtonian*

hedge fund

A private mutual fund which makes aggressive investments in the securities markets. Unlike conventional mutual funds, hedge funds can sell short, trade in options, and borrow money, thereby increasing their odds of beating the market. Hedge funds are attractive to the rich because they are unregulated—by limiting the number of investors to under one hundred, they escape SEC scrutiny—and secret: they are not required to report their activities to any governmental agency, are not listed in newspapers, and are prohibited from advertising. Most hedge funds require a minimum investment of $1 million.

inheritance tax
A dreaded confiscatory tax which has inspired all manner of legal ploys, dodges, machinations, and otherwise idiotic behavior.

in terrorem clause
A provision in a will requiring forfeiture of a specific bequest if the beneficiary unsuccessfully challenges the validity of the will.

junk bond
A high-yield, high-risk, and therefore low-rated corporate bond.
I really don't understand why 1,600 people have to be let go in Winston-Salem or the price of a box of Ritz Crackers has to go up thirty cents . . . in order to pay the junk-bond interest so that some clown can cut a swath in what passes for New York society.

MICHAEL M. THOMAS

kleptocracy
A government whose raison d'etre is to loot the national treasury. It runs the country like a racketeering enterprise, creating dummy corporations to exploit government contracts, transferring public funds

to personal bank accounts, and even abetting drug smuggling. Philippine President Ferdinand Marcos and his wife, Imelda, allegedly amassed a $5 billion fortune on his $25,000-a-year president's salary. Other kleptocrats include Juan and Eva Perón of Argentina, the shah of Iran, Manuel Noriega in Panama, and Papa Doc Duvalier (succeeded briefly by his son, Jean-Claude) in Haiti.

Leach, Robin

A British-born plutophile who has been dubbed "the Gulliver of Glitz" for his tireless peregrinations as the Champagne-wishes-and-caviar-dreams-host of *Lifestyles of the Rich and Famous,* a nationally syndicated chronicle of conspicuous consumption.

There's nothing wrong in being rich. There's a lot of things that rich people might do that are not right with the world, but there's an awful lot that they do that we don't know that they do.

ROBIN LEACH

limousine liberal

A term coined in the 1930s to describe an ostentatiously wealthy person who espouses traditionally liberal or Democratic causes. Roughly synonymous with "champagne socialist."

nouveau pauvre

"New poor"; the downwardly mobile rich.

For every gilded aristocrat chronicled in the gossip pages of the popular press, there is a less publicized peer or baronet living off the waning glory of his ancestral past. Some dwell in the crumbling wing of an Elizabethan manor, others have retreated to terraced houses in obscure London burroughs and others still are reduced to bedsits. . . . The NP may still own land, stocks in the family business (long since taken over) and a house filled with valuable antiques, but because of intractable trusts and complex laws of entailment, he is almost always legally denied the right to sell any or part of his inheritance for a reasonably profitable sum. His trust fund or annual allowance covers (not in all cases) the minimal costs of his life, yet he is still unable to afford to live in the style to which his progenitors were accustomed.

NICHOLAS MONSON AND DEBRA SCOTT, *The Nouveaux Pauvres: A Guide to Downward Nobility*

OCD
"Our class, dear."

pas devant les domestiques
"Not in front of the servants," a warning not to discuss a confidential matter in the presence of the help, who presumably do not understand French.

plutocracy
Government by the rich.
Obviously, in a plutocracy the natural hero is the man who robs a bank.

WILLIAM CARLOS WILLIAMS

plutography

Depiction of the lives of the very rich, as in novels, plays, movies, or on television. Tom Wolfe called the eighties the "Decade of Plutography":

Status is an influence at every level. We resist the notion that it matters, but it's true. You can't escape it. You see it in restaurants—not just in New York. People seem willing to pay any amount to be seen at this week's restaurant of the century. It's all part of what I call plutography: depicting the acts of the rich. They not only want to be seen at this week's restaurant of the century, they want to be embraced by the owner.

    TOM WOLFE

plutolatry*

The worship of wealth.

plutology*

The scientific study of wealth.

plutomania*

The abnormal or excessive desire for wealth; insane delusions of wealth.

*It is perhaps significant that these words generally do not appear in American dictionaries published after 1950.

Renoir clause

A provision in a prenuptial agreement stating that in case of divorce, the rich spouse's family heirlooms are not subject to distribution.

scion

An offshoot or twig; a child or descendant. For some reason the word is used almost exclusively to describe wealthy heirs (one seldom encounters the phrase, "*scion* of an average middle-class family").

significant wealth

According to investment advisors who service the very rich, a net worth of up to $100 million. Cf. *substantial wealth*.

substantial wealth

A net worth over $100 million. Cf. *significant wealth*.

social climber

One who strives for acceptance in fashionable society.

See that bivalve social climber
Feeding the rich Mrs. Hoggenheimer.
Think of his joy as he gaily glides
Down the middle of her gilded insides.
Proud little oyster.

COLE PORTER, *"The Tale of an Oyster"*

socialite

A journalistic euphemism for a rich person at a party.

The newspaper epithet socialite *requires no registration to back it up: Neither Blaine Trump nor Amanda Burden is listed [in the* Social Register*].*

NELSON W. ALDRICH, JR., *New York Magazine*

Social Register

A directory of prominent persons, called the "Stud Book" by those whose names appear in it.

stealth wealth

Status symbols which tend to avoid scrutiny. The backlash against the excesses of the 1980s sensitized the rich to the outrage of the middle-class, and to the danger from kidnappers, carjackers, tax collectors, and Rolex bandits. Conspicuous consumption has thus gone underground, and the rich have begun to choose four-wheel-drive vehicles over Rolls-Royces and industrial-grade brown diamonds over ostentatious sparklers.

summer

A verb peculiar to the rich.

Those who summer *on Fishers Island are the sort who expect their maid to die a week before they do in order to get things prepared in that happy hostelry in the sky.*

TAKI THEODORACOPULOS

sumptuary laws

Official regulation of personal expenditures, such as the French Socialist government's conspicuous consumption tax on "exterior signs of wealth."

The last time I was in Paris, I was always seeing liveried chauffeurs jumping out of tiny Fiats. I asked Paloma [Picasso] what was going on, and she told me the French have this tax on showing off. I was so amused. If anyone deserves to have showing off restricted, it's the French.

FRAN LEBOWITZ

total compensation

The entire "package" of remuneration paid to a corporate executive, including salary, bonuses, and stock options. In 1992, Walt Disney Chairman Michael Eisner cashed in the generous stock options he received when he joined the company in 1984, selling 3.5 million of his 5.4 million shares of Disney stock at a profit of $200 million, thereby earning more in one day than the average Disney employee earns in a lifetime.

trophy real estate

Property which somehow enhances the image of its owner. Donald Trump called the Plaza Hotel in New York "the ultimate trophy in the world" when he bought it for $325 million in 1988. He sold it in 1995 to a Saudi Prince and a Singapore developer for some $75 million less.

unit

Texas slang for $100 million.

walker

A term coined by *Women's Wear Daily* to describe a man who regularly escorts wealthy women to charity events when their husbands are unable or unwilling to accompany them.

[Jerome] Zipkin may be one of the most recognizable of the Walkers in Nouvelle Society, but he hardly invented the role. Society itself invented the Walker, specifically for the woman who, in spite of her wealth, finds herself lonely, with only a boring husband for company. Enter the Walkers, who can gossip, amuse, and advise on almost any subject under the sun, including how to entertain, whom to have for dinner, and the latest word on the latest fashions. They have even been known to provide hot tips on the stock market.

    JOHN FAIRCHILD, *Chic Savages*

WASP

The acronym for "White Anglo-Saxon Protestant"

What's so singularly equivocal about Wasps [is] that their status is grounded in the inheritance of wealth in a culture that is worshipful only of makers of it.

    NELSON W. ALDRICH, JR., *New York Magazine*

WASP Rot Syndrome

The decline in the wealth, status, and vitality of White Anglo-Saxon Protestants.

I have a confession: My family has a social disease. I call it the WASP Rot Syndrome. It is characterized by the slow erosion of ambition, energy, trust funds and SAT scores, a downward mobility that affects a whole class that once was accustomed to privilege and responsibility. The ancestors were judges, adventurers, tycoons; the progeny are drummers and day laborers. The grandparents served on charity boards in the city; the grandchildren live in cabins in the woods and, as a friend explained, "associate with people with no teeth."

. . . After several generations of slippage, many WASPs now spend much of their time twisting in the wind of mediocrity. Their houses are smaller than their grandparents'. So are their horizons. At their best, they are charming, reliable and civic-minded. At their worst, they are narrow, nasty, aimless and drink too much. In pop culture, they have been reduced to an ethnic joke, as in "How can you tell the bride at a WASP wedding?" "She's the one kissing the golden retriever."

ABIGAIL TRAFFORD, *Washington Post*

Index

Index

Index

243

Index

Index

Index

Index

About the editor

Jon Winokur is the author of various books, including The Portable Curmudgeon, Zen to Go, *and* Je Ne Sais What? *He lives in Pacific Palisades, California.*